THE SPHINX OF THE CHARLES

THE SPHINX OF THE CHARLES

A Year at Harvard with Harry Parker

TOBY AYER

LYONS
PRESS

Essex, Connecticut

An imprint of Globe Pequot, the trade division of
The Rowman & Littlefield Publishing Group, Inc.
4501 Forbes Blvd., Ste. 200
Lanham, MD 20706
www.rowman.com

Distributed by NATIONAL BOOK NETWORK

British Library Cataloguing in Publication Information Available

Library of Congress Cataloging-in-Publication Data

Names: Ayer, Toby, author.
Title: The sphinx of the Charles : a year at Harvard with Harry Parker / Toby Ayer.
Description: Guilford, Connecticut : Lyons Press, 2016. | Includes bibliographical references and
    index.
Identifiers: LCCN 2016014952 (print) | LCCN 2016028604 (ebook) | ISBN 9781493026531
    (hardcopy) | ISBN 9781493066407 (paperback) | ISBN 9781493026548 (e-book)
Subjects: LCSH: Parker, Harold Lambert, 1935-2013. | Ayer, Toby. | Harvard University—
    Rowing—History. | Rowing coaches—Massachusetts—Biography.
Classification: LCC GV790.92.P36 A94 2016 (print) | LCC GV790.92.P36 (ebook) | DDC
    797.12/30922—dc23
LC record available at https://lccn.loc.gov/2016014952

For my family,
and my rowing family

Contents

Thou hast taught me, Silent River!
Many a lesson, deep and long;
Thou hast been a generous giver;
I can give thee but a song.

TO THE RIVER CHARLES
HENRY WADSWORTH LONGFELLOW

Charles River Bridges & Boathouses

Main St. (99)

Austin St. (93)

Museum of Science

Community Sailing

Longfellow Bridge

Union BC

Cambridge Pkwy.

Monsignor O'Brien Hwy. (28)

3rd St.

Binney St.

Broadway

Main St.

Charles River

Race course

Beacon St.

Boylston St. (2)

(90)

Huntington Ave.

Cambridge Ave. (28)

Somerville Ave.

Cambridge St.

Hampshire St.

Windsor St.

CAMBRIDGE

Massachusetts Ave. Bridge

MIT

Washington St.

Prospect St.

Vassar St.

Storrow Dr.

(2)

Western Ave.

(2A)

River St.

Brookline St.

Putnam Ave.

BU

BU Bridge

Beacon St.

HARVARD

Riverside BC

(3) (2)

Powerhouse Stretch

Weld

Weeks Bridge

N. Harvard St.

(20)

Harvard St.

Newell

Stadium

Winchester St.

Brattle St.

(2)

Cambridge BC

Eliot Bridge

Greenough Blvd.

Coolidge Ave.

Soldier's Field Rd.

Western Ave.

Everett St.

(90)

(30)

Cambridge St.

Northeastern

Grove St.

Market St.

Mt. Auburn St.

Arsenal St.

N. Beacon St.

CRI (Harry Parker Boathouse)

0   0.5   1 km.
0   0.5   1 mi.

Foreword

I met Harry Parker early in January of 2000. I was in my fourth year of graduate school in England and intended to move back to the United States later that year. Harry's former boatman, Everett Abbot, had been in England helping Oxford with the rigging for some boats we were trying out, and he told me that Harry often had a coaching assistant and I should call him. It happened that my grandfather passed away near Christmas, and I flew back to Boston for the memorial service. While in town, I walked into Newell Boathouse and introduced myself to Harry and Bill Manning, who were working in the office. That spring Harry e-mailed me to say that I could have the job. His wife Kathy joked later that maybe it was "because of the beard," though I think I grew mine first.

Of course I knew of Harry by reputation, especially having rowed at MIT for four years. I have a memory of him at the indoor rowing championships in 1996, carrying young Abigail in a backpack. Over the course of the year when I was Harry's coaching assistant, I felt gradually welcomed fully into the family at Newell Boathouse. I have never felt out of place there, despite not being a Harvard rower. Harry, Charley, Bill, Blocker, Linda, Joe, Wayne, and the rowers—all of them made me feel at home. In 2003, the night before the National Championship finals, Harry offered me the extra bed in his hotel room. (I accepted. He watched some baseball. The air-conditioning was very cold.) In 2006 I drove to Gales Ferry to watch The Race against Yale in the early morning, after it had been postponed from the night before. After it was over, I walked up to the dining hall, intending just to poke my head in for a second. The team was sitting down for their year-end banquet, also postponed. One of the coxswains saw me and said, "grab a plate." When Harry's illness became widely known, and the alumni compiled a book of messages to him, my short contribution was on the theme of generosity. I owe everyone at Newell an enormous debt of gratitude for the privilege of spending so much time there.

I started thinking about this book that first year with Harry, and began writing down little scenes as they happened, moments that I felt were never captured in the usual descriptions in books or the press pieces that appeared about Harry. He had been a figure—a looming, important figure—in other books, but it seemed to me that he deserved some time and space exclusively for himself, and no one had done it. Who could do it? Harry was capable of writing his own story (though perhaps, had he done so, it would have been too brief), but when I told Harry I was interested in writing about him, he said he had no plans to write his own memoir. As for my own project, he said he was "not, on the face of it, totally opposed to the idea." I took that as great encouragement and so, during the academic year (2007–08) described in these chapters, in between teaching two classes at MIT, I went over to Harvard a few times a week, got as close to Harry as seemed appropriate, and wrote down or recorded what I could. Harry just gave me a seat and talked with me at his pleasure. I have not "recreated" any dialogue or quotations. If something appears in quotation marks, then someone said it and I wrote it down, or it was quoted as such elsewhere.

This is not a biography. It is more of an extended profile, with flashbacks and reflections on Harry's rowing life. I do not have grand things to say about Harry, or ways to explain his character based on his formative years. I would have loved to speak with his siblings or crewmates or his college coach, and to read his childhood writings. But mostly I wanted to record more of the Harry Parker I knew, to show those in the rowing world a bit more than what they thought they knew, to complete the picture.

Mostly I have tried to keep myself out of the story, but you may imagine me sitting next to Harry in the launch, on a bench on the dock or a chair in the tank room, spinning along on an erg while his team does their afternoon workout, or standing with a crew by the trailer before they head out to race.

Introduction: Harry Parker and the Cauldron of Pain

The November 15, 1968 edition of *Time* magazine was a post-election issue with Richard Nixon on the cover. Amid the political analysis was a piece on the fine art of losing entitled "Sweet and Sour Grapes," which ended with a list of quotations from Nixon, William Jennings Bryan, Napoleon, Socrates, and others. Vince Lombardi had left the Green Bay Packers the year before, and his now-famous line was there: "Winning is not the most important thing about football—it's the only thing." Next after Lombardi was a US Olympic coach consoling his team: "There's nothing wrong with being the sixth best in the world," he said. The coach was Harry Parker, and the team was his heavyweight crew from Harvard, who had just finished last in the Olympic final. Despite Parker's consolation, there had been high expectations for that crew. Decades later he was still sure that, had they not been sick from the high altitude of Mexico City, his eight would have won the Olympics.

Three years earlier, Parker had been on the front cover of *Sports Illustrated* looking boyish in a red polo shirt and short hair, smiling with arms crossed, his varsity boat rowing across the background. They were labeled "the world's best crew." It has been a while since Parker, or American rowing in general, has had that sort of coverage. (When Harvard was building its football stadium in 1904, some thought it was unseemly to encourage the public to watch the college games; one rebuttal to this qualm was that the new stadium would be for the college and not for the public, to whom "rowing is more important than football." Imagine!)

Though not in the mainstream spotlight, Harvard rowing has maintained an incredible record of success, and Harry Parker remained behind the megaphone until he passed away in 2013, at age seventy-seven. Forty years after that *Sports Illustrated* cover, Parker's varsity crew was so good they were allowed into a major international regatta as a second-string USA entry. They made the finals and finished fifth, beating several national teams. A year later the team captain, counting his blessings for a reporter, pointed to being coached by "the most important man in the sport."

Not only did Parker dominate the college rowing scene from the 1960s on, he essentially invented the current model of college rowing in America. When he started coaching Harvard freshmen in 1961, there was a bit of rowing in the fall, occasional and brief visits to the rowing tanks in the winter, and then the spring racing season from April to June. Athletes could pursue other sports in the other seasons the way they did, and still do, in high school. Parker took over the varsity in the spring of 1963 after his predecessor Harvey Love died of a heart attack. It had been a lackluster season: Harvard did not even qualify for the six-boat final at the Eastern Sprints championship in May, and Yale would presumably beat them for a second time at their traditional private match ("The Race") on the Thames River in New London. But Parker started training them differently, based on a German model of low-cadence work. They rebuilt their entire rhythm from scratch. After upsetting Yale that year, Harvard beat them for the next seventeen years, and did not lose to *any* college for five years. The varsity eight made the finals at the Sprints for the next forty-five years without fail, and won it more than any other team. Much more. (During Parker's coaching career, Yale and Pennsylvania each won four Sprints titles; Princeton, five; Brown, seven; and Harvard, twenty-three.)

The British magazine *Rowing* tried to explain in 1965 how Harvard had suddenly put themselves "in an entirely different class from other American crews . . . One begins to feel a certain compassion for those who must row against them." The article's analysis was a hodgepodge, but it coalesced around the person of Harry Parker: "remarkable coaching skills . . . unique influence . . . fervent zeal . . . catalytic blend of tradition, innovation, and hard work . . . his own example."

Harry Parker was not a chatty man. He was described in 2000 as having "an impenetrable mystique." Since he made no attempt to explain himself, legends grew readily. David Halberstam wrote in *The Amateurs* in 1984 that Parker was "as much myth as man." Harvard's success under his guidance was so quick and so overwhelming that it seemed magical. *Sports Illustrated*'s Hugh Whall saw "a wordless rapport between this man and the men who row for him."

He had other powers, too. He heard everything and knew everything his oarsmen were doing. He could walk on water. He could control the weather. He was immaculately conceived, and he got younger as decades went by. In the early years he told a reporter that before a race, "generally, all I have to do is push a button." Every other coach must have wondered, mused the reporter, "where can he get a button like Harry Parker's?" A decade into his career, Parker's athletes had become acolytes. "We'd do anything for him," said Rick Grogan in 1974. "We'd walk off cliffs for him."

The press have described Parker as "a master of understatement," "modest to a fault," "always intimidating," "courtly," "patrician," "taciturn," "deep-voiced," "a strikingly fit and youthful sexagenarian," "the Ancient Mariner of the college crew fraternity," "a reluctant hero," "seemingly incapable of hyperbole," "a god to his young men."

Despite decades of scrutiny, the mystique was ever-present, even in relatively lean years for Harvard (though Parker coached exactly one losing season). In 1996, Yale managed a rare "sweep" of all four races at the Harvard-Yale Regatta in early summer (rare, that is, for Yale), and the Yale varsity were favored to repeat in 1997, having beaten Harvard twice over the usual racing distance of two kilometers (a mile and a quarter). But The Race is longer—four miles—and a good 2k crew isn't always the same as a good four-mile crew. And Parker produced great four-mile crews.

A reporter at the finish line overheard the remarks of two Harvard alumni, as the Crimson crossed the flags a length ahead of Yale. Class of 1950: "Guess Harry waved his magic wand again." Class of '52: "You're right. He did."

⌒

Apart from Parker's personal example as a model of competitiveness and zeal, perhaps his most crucial early initiative was persuading his rowers, as the magazine *Rowing* put it, "to engage with enthusiasm in an almost forbiddingly intense program of year-round training." Top-level collegiate rowing soon became a sport that began in September and ended in June. Ivy League rules regarding water-time notwithstanding, the oarsmen at Harvard are out in boats until the end of November, and back on the water whenever the springtime ice clears—and sometimes before. In between they train indoors on weights, in artificial rowing tanks, and on the rowing ergometer, or "erg." This is the same device found in health clubs everywhere, the standard machine worldwide, made by the Morrisville, Vermont, company Concept II. It mimics the rowing stroke with a sliding seat, a handle attached by a chain to a flywheel, and a little screen that tells you how fast you are going. Rowers spend endless hours watching those little screens, maintaining their five-hundred-meter split times that are updated after each stroke, aware of each second on the clock, each meter that ticks away, doing mental "erg math" to occupy the mind until the body can rest.

One of Parker's 1968 Olympic crew described the sport of rowing as "a struggle to force yourself into a cauldron of pain." The erg is perceived in the rowing world as the perfect device to facilitate that struggle: It produces all the physical anguish of rowing without the distraction of scenery or the useful foci of other bodies to sync with and other crews to compete with. A more recent Harvard grad contrasted rowing with bicycling: Since a bike race is so long, you try to go fast without hurting yourself; but in a rowing race, which is essentially a long sprint, you need to hurt yourself as soon as possible, and then hang on.

The standard race distance of 2,000 meters usually takes somewhere around six minutes to complete (novices are closer to seven minutes, whereas the world record for a men's eight is less than five and a half). To go at maximum speed for this amount of time requires a mixture of aerobic and anaerobic ability, and they combine in a grueling fashion. Crews burst furiously off the line, and while the first several seconds are painless and exhilarating, the body is put immediately into oxygen debt with several minutes of supreme effort still to come—and it soon becomes apparent. The propulsive phase of the rowing stroke begins with a compressed, crouching position, and then the body opens up by pushing the legs and drawing back the torso; the arms pull toward the body to finish off the stroke. It is a lot like a power clean in weightlifting. Do this between thirty and forty times a minute for six minutes and you will tire out nearly all of your body's muscles. Your lungs will burn and you may taste blood. You will feel the sting of lactic acid in your legs, forearms, and rear end. The bottoms of your feet may burn, too—some rowers dangle them in the water after a race. Learning to live in this cauldron of pain is part of learning to row.

Parker didn't favor the emphasis on pain in rowing. He preferred the notion "fatigue management." Not that he spent much time discussing fatigue management strategies with his athletes. Their daily workouts tested and developed both physiology and psychology, and they learned their own coping methods. A given piece of work might be described as "two-thirds power," or "three-quarters power," but Parker never defined those levels for the rowers. They figured it out, he said. Before an erg test (at a set distance: 10k, 5k, 2k, etc.), Parker would talk to them quietly and urge a cautious approach. He would tell them to find a pace they could maintain for the whole distance, to leave room to go faster at the end.

And that, typically, is what Harvard crews have done. In that miraculous 1963 Harvard-Yale win, Parker's crew trailed Yale for nearly half the race, then passed them and kept moving. Fifty years later they still won many of their races with this pattern: Even if the final margin was enormously lopsided in Harvard's favor, they often trailed at the start. But Parker had trained them all year with "building pieces"—set lengths of work that start at one cadence and intensity and then increase throughout. They might start at two-thirds pressure, increase to three-quarters, and finally to 90 percent. Whether the pieces were two minutes, ten minutes, or twenty minutes, they would usually have a building profile. And if possible, another crew would be alongside rowing neck-and-neck (more properly, "bowball to bowball"), or chasing them from behind, or starting ahead as a goal to catch.

Parker introduced building pieces to his crews in the 1970s. Until then, all rowing training was done at full pressure. Crews would row a little with only part of the crew (by fours or sixes) to start, but there was nothing referred to as a "warmup." "Every time you rowed all eight, you started rowing full pressure," he recalled. They would do pieces at twenty-two or twenty-four strokes per minute in the fall, and then at twenty-eight, thirty, or more in the spring, always racing other crews of their teammates. "It was either full pressure or paddling." Wednesdays were usually time-trials for Saturday's race, and sometimes, on Thursdays, they would have an "off" or "light" day: six times three-quarters of a mile—each piece of work lasting about four minutes—at twenty-six strokes per minute. This is not really a light workout, but at least they weren't racing other boats. One year he tried having a crew row at three-quarter power so he could focus on a technical point without the pressure of all-out racing. Later he tried building pieces, and they became his mainstay training tool.

A race is in many ways just another workout. Parker did not provide a stroke-by-stroke race plan. Nor would he deliver a big speech before they hit the water. Rather he exhorted, on a daily basis, a universal attitude to adopt, and the attitude was: "Be stubborn!" On the morning of a race day in the spring, when his crews arrived at Newell Boathouse, Parker was typically miles downstream on the racecourse. They would find a piece of paper tacked to the bulletin board in the locker room, with a scrawled message from Parker in blue Sharpie pen. "Great Day!" it would say at the top. It might not say anything else, other than a time for them to launch the boat for their race. If there was more, it would be simple: be aggressive, race the whole distance, stay strong. Parker would have suggested some ten-stroke bursts of effort (known as "power tens") at a few set points in the race, but for the most part the rowers and the coxswain worked out any other details themselves. The race was in their hands.

In 2005 both Harvard and Princeton had very good crews, and they faced each other three times: in their regular dual meet in April, again at the Eastern Sprints, and finally at the Intercollegiate Rowing Association regatta in June—the National Championships. At the big regattas, races are six boats across—you can see your opponents to your left and right and sense the relative speeds of the crews as you creep ahead or fall behind. In that IRA final, the University of California–Berkeley took an early lead on all crews, with Harvard and Princeton level and half a boat-length behind. It took 1,500 meters, three-quarters of the race, for

Harvard to grind back that half-length and take the lead, with Princeton always next to them, only two seats down. Harvard won the race, to take their third consecutive national championship. Here is a conversation between Harry Parker and a reporter afterward:

> *Reporter*: These races against Princeton are not for the faint of heart.
>
> *Parker*: No, they sure aren't, they sure aren't. It's a very, very strong crew, Princeton.
>
> *Reporter*: It seems to me in a race like this, it has to be a tactical race.
>
> *Parker*: You know, it really isn't. You just have to go as hard as you can. Both crews are so strong, so steady, there are no weaknesses, you just row as hard as you can and hope you get there.
>
> *Reporter*: But you have to know how long you can go all out.
>
> *Parker*: No, you just go. Go until you can't go any more.

Fifty years after Harvard took him on, Harry Parker's varsity crew won the marquee Championship Eight event at the Head of the Charles to start their year, and then won the Ladies' Challenge Plate at Henley to finish it. In 2013, weakened by myelodysplastic syndrome, Parker drove his own launch to watch his nearly unbeaten squad complete yet another sweep of Yale at The Race in Gales Ferry, Connecticut. The following weekend he spent an afternoon on the water with his 1980 Olympic eight. Two days later he passed away. Parker was following his own advice.

Another Great Year

MORE THAN ANYTHING ELSE, THE CHARLES IS A ROWING RIVER. WHENever it is not frozen solid, and even when early-spring ice floes are still drifting downstream toward Boston Harbor, there is usually someone rowing on the Charles. In late December you may see footprints in the snow on a launching dock, showing where a sculler carried his boat down to the freezing water. In February, when a small patch of free water opens up downstream on the Cambridge shore, you may look out from the window of the Red Line as you cross the Longfellow Bridge and see that someone, somehow, has found a place to put in and is now sculling back and forth, back and forth, two minutes at a time, not to miss the opportunity to be on the water. Under normal conditions, rowers contend with fishing boats, canoes and kayaks, duck boats, pleasure yachts, the big tour boats that leave from Science Park, a Venetian-style gondola, and sailboats—all on the same stretch of water where the college crews hold their spring races. The presence of sailing suggests that Boston isn't the best place for rowing, since wind creates rough water, and rough water may be deemed "unrowable." Rowers and their coaches are always thinking about wind conditions, deciding where to go for the day's practice session. Upstream, west and north from the racecourse, the Charles bends and folds back on itself several times. As the river's axis changes direction, and buildings and trees and seawalls create shelters from the wind, some stretches of river will be placid even when others are choppy. Usually you can find someplace to row. Harvard University has two boathouses for rowing, one for the men and one for the women, on opposite sides of the river near the Lars Anderson Bridge, just down the street from Harvard Square. With the two biggest bends in the river just above and below, and a few miles of water in either direction, Harvard is well placed to find rowable water close to home.

If you spend time along the banks of the Charles with your eyes open, you start to recognize some characters: the man who spends late afternoons with his drum set, perched on the Cambridge shore just below the Riverside Boat Club; the young man with long hair and a backpack, walking down the path on the Boston side wearing his headphones and singing along, loudly and out of tune; the two Asian women with blonde hair (twin sisters?), running side-by-side in Boston Marathon jackets; the Native American man with long graying hair, also a runner, inevitably dubbed "the Chief" by Harvard students.

If you look down to the river itself, you could easily find familiar figures there, too. You might recognize the wiry man who sculls his single from far upstream, often with no shirt, or some of the Riverside scullers with blue and white stripes on their oar blades and shirts. For a couple of years, you would have seen the Winklevoss twins in matching yellow boats, followed by their own miniature coach driving a miniature launch. In the larger team boats there are too many faces and bodies to recognize easily, and they change from year to year, though you might learn to recognize the team blade designs (a big "T" on the MIT blades, a diagonal red/white split for Boston University, black and white and red for Northeastern, red with white tips for Harvard, not to mention several more colleges, high schools, and clubs). But the coaches often remain, and it is easy to recognize one, alone in a motor launch behind a crew. You might even learn their voices, as heard through a megaphone or electronic bullhorn.

On a September day in 2005, afternoon classes were meeting and rowing teams were out on the water. Harold Lambert Parker, coach of men's rowing at Harvard, well versed in wind and wave and oar, drove his launch upriver and explained to me why he stopped riding the Mount Washington bicycle race. He had done it four years in a row, the last two in very bad weather conditions. In 2003 there were 60-mph winds, and he almost got blown off his bike. He had a slight case of pneumonia right afterward, and wonders if he had started to feel it during the climb.

Mount Washington is the highest peak in New England at 6,288 feet, and there is an annual bike-race up the access road. The steepness, or grade, of a road is given as a percentage, the ratio of height gained to distance traveled on the road. Highways are rarely allowed to be more than 6 percent. San Francisco's famous Lombard Street is just over 14. Biking up a 3 percent grade will make you sweat after a couple of minutes, and 8 will make most people get off and push. The Col de la Madeleine in the Tour de France averages 8 percent for twelve miles. The Mount Washington road reverses these figures, averaging 12 percent for nearly eight miles. There are extended sections of 18 percent, and the last fifty yards are more than 22. Parker said he naively thought he could get up to speed early in the climb, and then sit back a little and grind away. He soon realized this was impossible: You just have to sprint the whole way. His first year in the race he finished second in his age group with a time of ninety-two minutes, and then won it for the next two years.

After four races, exhausted by the ride and threatened by the weather, Parker decided he'd had enough. "I realized that bad conditions are the norm. I was lucky the first two years." At the 2000 race the weather was "cool and misty . . . it was 32 degrees at the top. I had frostbite on my feet." Lucky! Next year, Parker will be seventy.

It is hard to characterize Parker's coaching career without sounding cliché, because so many people have said so much about it for so long. To describe it as the stuff of legend would simply be true, since there are legends. He was known for his personal competitiveness, unabated after so many decades. He was thought to be gruff and dismissive, awkward and distant. He was feared and loved. His reputation, of course, was tied to that of his crews: Harvard was not always the fastest varsity crew in the country, but rarely were they far off. They were known for their tenacity, their consistency, their ability to come back when they were down and win. They did this from the moment Parker started coaching them, and they still did it fifty years later.

Here are some things Parker's oarsmen have said:

"Everyone who ever met Harry Parker said there was some sort of aura about him."

"He doesn't always explain what he's doing, he just does it. You don't completely understand what's going on in his head, but you trust what comes out of it."

"Harry's force of personality is so strong that he brings confidence in any situation."

"He's like the Alan Greenspan of rowing. We hang on every word he says."

"He's deadly honest. He's never tried to psych us, or insult us with a pep talk."

"I used to go for weeks and Harry would never say anything to me."

"He was a master manipulator."

"He's the best—a real man of integrity."

"He is the most competitive human being I've ever met, period."

"I have been very successful in my life, and the teacher/mentor was Harry."

"You'd hear that low, deep voice coming at you across the water, and it would send a shiver down your spine."

"Harry must be the best coach in the whole wide world."

"Having been forged in Harry's fire, tackling life's other challenges doesn't seem so hard."

At England's prestigious Henley Royal Regatta, the Grand Challenge Cup is typically contested by national teams from various countries. The last time a college crew won the Grand, it was Harvard. On the wall upstairs at Newell Boathouse, in a large frame, is a set of race photos and pages from the 1985 regatta program, commemorating the achievement. At the bottom is hand-lettered: HARRY L. PARKER, HARVARD UNIVERSITY HEAD CREW COACH, 1963 ∞. It was written less than halfway through his career.

In the fall of 2005, two decades after that Henley win, the Harvard heavyweight team had inherited a reputation of invincibility. The last few graduating classes jokingly called themselves the God Squad: "Half of us believe in God, the other half think we *are* gods," said one. (Three from the 2004 crew—of the latter persuasion, it turns out—rowed at the 2008 Olympics.) This God Squad won three consecutive Eastern Sprints titles and three consecutive National Championships. They won three events in the same year at the Henley Royal Regatta, an incredible show of strength. In one event at Henley, the final race was between two Harvard crews. Most races had enormous margins of victory, even the championships. Two lengths, three lengths, twenty seconds. The 2003 junior varsity crew stumbled early in the Grand Final of the Eastern Sprints and found themselves down by over a boat-length to Princeton; they came back to win the race, with clear water between them and the Tigers.

After three years of winning just about everything, nearly unchallenged, what do you say to your team as they begin the new year? When they came back to the boathouse in September, they found a message tacked to the bulletin board in the heavyweight locker room, essentially the same one that had appeared every fall. A white piece of paper with Parker's blue-Sharpie scrawl: "Welcome back! Let's make 2005–6 another great year for Harvard crew!" Before their first row on the water, he had talked to the rowers for a couple of minutes, telling them that he was excited about the year, but there were other programs in the country that would be very strong. He expected they knew which ones: Princeton and California. And that was it. They went rowing.

Two weeks later, an eight-man crew was warming up, with only six of them rowing as Parker's coaching launch followed them upstream from Newell Boathouse and around the long oxbow turn toward Eliot Bridge. His crews followed the same warmup pattern daily, whether for a normal practice or a race. It was a simple progression of stroke-length, effort, and boat speed, and it was effective. After pushing off from the dock, they crossed the river to head upstream. Starting with half the boat, either the stern four or the bow four, the coxswain (who sits in the stern, steers the boat, and gives commands through a microphone) had them first row whaleboat-style with just their arms and body, then add more and more length to the stroke by letting the seat roll forward and then pushing with the legs: first a quarter-slide, then half-slide, and finally full slide, maybe twenty strokes of each, and all with their blades squared up, leaving the crimson-and-white blade pattern displayed like flags as they swung back from the "finish" to the "catch." Parker didn't talk to them as they did this; in fact he usually caught up to them only after they'd finished the warmup. During these few minutes the rowers eased into the rowing motion, paid attention to each part of the stroke, started getting used to each other and the timing of their motions.

After the fours, depending on their instructions, the crew would either turn and head back downstream or keep going up, but now rowing by sixes, with blades feathering and squaring. The boat was moving faster now, requiring more responsiveness, a quicker application of the oar to the water flowing by, in order to push against it. After rowing for a minute or so at a low, steady pace—two-thirds pressure, perhaps eighteen strokes per minute—the coxswain called for a ten-stroke burst at three-quarter pressure at a higher stroke-rate, maybe twenty-two or twenty-four. Then the cox switched pairs so a different combination of six are rowing ("bow pair in, three and four out," for instance) and the sequence repeated. With two rowers sitting by as dead weight, and two blades dragging across the water the whole time, the boat was slower and much more stable than it would be when all eight rowed. And once they did row with all eight, there would be a few more tens or twenties, gradually working up to the speed and intensity of that day's workout.

In a few places, especially in England, rivers are small enough and busy enough that rowing coaches do their work from a bicycle on shore. But usually it is from a motorboat, and most coaching launches are now "wakeless": The outboard motor is nestled between two pontoons, so its wake gets damped down and other crews aren't consigned to rowing in bouncy water and waves that break over the gunwales, to slosh around in their boats and slow them down. Parker's launch had the pontoons, but it was not quite wakeless, and it was one of the largest on the Charles. The pontoons were white, and a faded red windbreak sat on the platform in between, with two folding chairs behind it. A full park bench was planted in the rear to accommodate more passengers.

The launch usually stayed fifteen feet or more off the stern of the crew, sometimes directly behind, sometimes at an oblique angle to one side or the other. Every so often, maybe twice a minute, Parker would raise his megaphone to his mouth and talk to a rower or the coxswain, then place it back down behind him. His megaphone was a long white plastic one, worn and frayed at the wide end. These megaphones come with little metal handles, like screen-door handles, but Parker's had a wooden "pistol-grip" screwed on, painted crimson.

As Harry headed upstream, another Harvard crew passed coming down, at the end of their own workout, followed by Bill Manning, the heavyweight freshmen coach. Until recently all college rowing programs divided the freshmen—both the experienced and the true novices—from the varsity, and had separate coaches for each group. In Bill's launch was a rowing prospect, a high school senior interested in coming to Harvard. Since the boy would be hosted that night by one of the varsity rowers and they needed to meet up after practice, the two coaches eased their launches together and he stepped across. He took the seat next to Harry as I moved to the bench behind.

In the middle of the river, following the crew again upstream above Eliot Bridge, Parker suddenly searched from pocket to pocket in his shirt and trousers, then fished out his cell phone and called the boathouse: He didn't have his wedding ring. He told whoever answered the phone that between going sculling earlier and getting dressed again, his ring didn't end up on his finger. Parker typically trained in his single scull during the summer and fall, leading up to the Head of the Charles Regatta in late October. "I'm pretty sure the sequence was bench, desk, locker room," he said, meaning the workbench in the shop, next to the rack there where his sculling boat lives. He didn't actually ask whoever it was to look for the ring; of course they would. On land, if Parker wanted to talk with you, he would say your name while approaching, and then look away as his right hand pointed at you with knuckles down and his forefinger beckoned you, curling in twice. He would walk on, and you were to follow. Bill Manning said that when work needed to be done, anyone nearby became a body, a laborer—no matter if you were a rower, coach, or innocent bystander.

The phone went away, he glanced at the crew, and the megaphone came up again as he addressed a rower in the middle of the boat: "Keep your hands lower until you square the blade, so it doesn't scrape the water early . . . no, you're raising them too soon; keep them low, square, *then* raise them . . . that's the idea." When he talked with the recruit in the launch, Parker turned on the bright charm that was mostly reserved for high school students, and was played to its limit at the rowing camp he ran every summer. "Sorry about the weather! Usually it's much better this time of year!" It was in fact a glorious, sunny, late-summer Boston day. The boy was a little nervous and kept calling Parker "sir," and it sounded jarring every time. Newspapers and magazines called him "Parker," of course. Rowers of the past nicknamed him "Weird Harold," "The Weird One," "The Old PF," even "God," and in latter days they referred to him casually as "HP," but he was never "sir" or even "Coach." Everyone on the river called him "Harry."

Two years later, in the fall of 2007, another crop of freshmen are getting oriented to campus, Harvard Square, Cambridge, and Boston. Harry's crews the last two years have been strong, *very* strong, but not national champions: fourth in the country in 2006 (sure enough, behind Cal, Princeton, and Brown) and third in 2007. Last spring they lost to Princeton on the Charles for the first time in fifty years. They lost to Yale by an inconceivable half-second over four miles, their first loss in "The Race" in eight years. But Harry's squad has nonetheless dominated. They still win team point trophies at major regattas, and the varsity won the Eastern Sprints, which bought them another trip to the Henley Royal Regatta. Which they won.

Classes will start soon, some sports are already in full swing, and informational posters crowd the bulletin boards around campus. Among them are the crew fliers: 8½" by 11" paper in landscape format, slightly glossy, a crimson background with a small white border, white lettering, sans serif, all caps:

FIND OUT HOW YOU CAN BE PART OF HARVARD'S
OLDEST AND MOST SUCCESSFUL SPORT FROM
THE FRESHMAN AND VARSITY COACHING STAFF AT THE

CREW MEETING

ALL INTERESTED CANDIDATES—NO EXPERIENCE NECESSARY
FRESHMAN ROWERS, COXSWAINS, AND MANAGERS
MEN AND WOMEN
HEAVYWEIGHTS AND LIGHTWEIGHTS

WEDNESDAY, SEPT. 12

5:30–6:00 PM AT THE SCIENCE CENTER

It is the same flier as last year, except for the date, and the same flier as ten years ago, except for the location. On Wednesday, as students enter the science center, assistant coach Blocker Meitzen catches their eye, asks if they are here for the crew meeting, and if so which squad, and directs them to the appropriate room. Upstairs in a classroom, perhaps three dozen prospective rowers are at the men's heavyweight meeting. There are no prospective managers. On the walls of the heavyweight lounge at Newell Boathouse, the last team photo that includes a "manager" is from 1978.

In front of the freshmen at their desks stand Harry, Bill, Wayne Berger (Harry's assistant with the varsity team for the last few years), the team captain, and the MP. The "Master of Protocol" is an elected position with a certain social authority among the heavyweights, a leadership role differentiated from the captain. The MP has power to set certain behavioral guidelines for the team, which are posted for the benefit of the freshmen. The canonical punishment from the MP is a dunk in the Charles, though cold water or a high bacterial count can stay the execution of justice. When Harry posts crew listings for practice, instead of their actual names, the MP may be denoted "MP," and the captain "CP."

The meeting is for the freshmen, so Bill Manning emcees in his cheerful, loud manner. He introduces Harry.

Harry is wearing a polo shirt, khaki trousers, and a baseball cap. A thin, light-brown beard traces his jaw, and the cap hides the fact that the top of his head is mostly bald. He speaks for a couple of minutes, standing mostly in one place, sometimes stepping slightly forward, then slightly back. His hands are in his pockets or on his hips. He says he is glad to see them all, and he hopes that they will have an "enjoyable, satisfying, and *successful*" rowing experience at Harvard. He points to the fact that they have been national champions three of the last five years, "not to boast, but to let you know the sort of success the program has had." He talks slowly, sometimes pausing, in a low, near-monotone with an occasional word emphasized. He is positive but not selling snake-oil. The message is: If you work hard, rowing will reward you. "Welcome!"

Bill takes over again and goes over bureaucratic details: swim test, physical, NCAA clearance, date and time of the first practice. He reassures them that Harvard lets the other teams get up early to row; Harvard practices in the afternoon. Here is what the team has ahead of them: practice with the team, nearly every day they are on campus this year, sometimes twice a day. Three or four "head races" in the fall, three-mile time-trials often on curvy stretches of various rivers. Two months of winter training on the rowing machines, indoor tanks, and weights, broken up by a training trip to Florida in January. A series of 2,000-meter "cup races" in the spring against other university crews from the Northeast, the same schedule as every year. The league championship in Worcester, known as the Eastern Sprints, and then, two weeks later, the National Championship regatta, called the IRA. And finally, in early June, The Race against Yale. Hours and hours and hours of training, for about a dozen total races in the whole year. The official "season" takes place on four Saturday mornings, and will last a cumulative total of less than half an hour.

When Bill starts talking, Harry walks out the door into the hallway, paces a little, stands quietly nearby, looking at the floor. And then the meeting is over. As the crowd of students streams by he smiles, shakes hands, smiles and says "welcome back!" or "good to see you!" or "there he is!" (The last is one of his favorite generic greetings.) He goes back into the room and fields questions with the others.

I join the Harvard coaches for dinner at John Harvard's Brew House after the meeting.

There are some new coaches on staff at Weld, the women's boathouse. Liz O'Leary, the women's head coach for the last twenty years, arrives with Weld's new boat-repairwoman, and Michelle Guerette appears with her boyfriend. Michelle rowed at Harvard, and has since become the best woman sculler in the country. She came back a few days ago from a bronze-medal performance at the World Championships (the following summer, she will win silver in Beijing). Harry is seated with a view of the Red Sox game on the big screen behind the bar. A young coaching assistant from the women's team is sitting next to him, and he talks with her, but often he is quiet and seems to pay more attention to the game than anything else. As the meal winds down, and Harry leaves to get home to his family, it emerges that he has paid the entire bill. When O'Leary is told this, she raises her eyebrows and stares for a few seconds, shocked.

Bill Manning, Wayne Berger, and Blocker Meitzen are all at the dinner, but the lightweight coaches didn't make it. Charley Butt, a thoughtful, witty ex–national team rower with a talent for technical coaching and miracle results, has coached the varsity lightweights since 1987 to extraordinary success. His freshman coach is Linda Muri, an MIT aeronautics grad with a decade of national team experience, who took over that post from Blocker Meitzen. Since then, Blocker has been back with the heavyweights, helping Harry with the lower varsity boats and Bill with the novices. The walk-on rowers and the recruited, experienced ones are kept apart for a month or more, until the novices have started to learn this new, unfamiliar skill. The gap between them can be large. Bill has been a prodigious recruiter, and his freshman classes typically include several members of junior national teams from this country and abroad; the novices, meanwhile, may never have seen a rowing shell. Also absent from dinner is Joe Shea, the boatman at Newell. When Joe first came to the boathouse, Harry told him he expected to be around for two or three more years. Ten years later Harry is still here, and so is Joe. He seems part of the woodwork.

—— ——

This year, there is no message on the board encouraging the team to make it "another great year for Harvard crew." On the afternoon of the year's first practice, it is business as usual. The lineup for the 2:30 practice was e-mailed to the team earlier in the day. On the bulletin board, the day's workout announcement is tacked up. "Great Day!" says the top of the sheet. And then:

Warm-up: CII 5'

OTW!

Post: 2x10 jumpsquats, 2x10 back extensions, CII 10' @ ¾ power

"CII" refers to the ergometer made by Concept II, hence the abbreviation, and "OTW" means "on the water." The post-row workout is a light one—the number of jumpsquats will multiply several times over the coming weeks.

From 2:20 on, rowers drift into the boathouse, change into Lycra unisuits, row for a few minutes on the ergs, and then gravitate to the lounge to talk and stretch on the wrestling-mat floor. At three o'clock, Harry pokes his head into the lounge. "Are we ready to go? . . . two or three minutes, okay?" The coxswain starts motivating the rowers to head downstairs to the boat bay. Harry is there, and leads them to one of the racks of oars, which are propped vertically with the blades down and the handles extending up to the ceiling. He indicates a set of oars for the crew to use, then wanders from one bay to the next, rowers and coxswain trailing behind, inspecting the various Pocock training hulls. These are the old, heavy, stable boats the team will use for a few weeks as they get used to rowing again. It looks like he hasn't thought about what equipment they will be using until this very moment. When he finally settles on one the rowers look at it, glance at the interior, and joke about whether the shoes will be usable. Some of these boats have full shoes screwed into place, which is the norm, but some just have a plate with a heel cup and two laced flaps to hold each foot in.

Joe is tinkering with a launch at the upstream edge of the dock. A rower carries two oars down—one port, one starboard—leaves them on the dock, and says hi to Joe. Just then, a water bottle skitters down the wooden planks: A common game among the rowers is to see how close they can get their bottles to the water without them falling in, and this is the first one of the year. It skids, slows, rolls sideways onto the flat section of dock near Joe, and plops into the water to gleeful cries from other rowers carrying oars. One of them fishes it out.

Once they have carried their boat down to the water, fixed their oars into the oarlocks, and are adjusting their shoe positions, Harry walks over to tell the coxswain what to do: fours up, spin, run through the normal fours sequence a second time coming downstream. Then to everyone: "Alright? Here we go!" He goes back up to the shop and reappears with his megaphone, seat cushions for the launch, an extra jacket, a sandwich, and tea in a travel mug. The engine gives him some trouble on starting and he has to play with the choke and let it run for a few minutes. Typically Harry can time all this preparation so that he backs the launch away from the dock just as the crew emerges from around the Eliot bend and nears the boathouse again. But now they aren't in sight, and he glances up and down the river. "Where are they? I guess we should go find them." As soon as the launch pulls out, they appear upriver.

When they finish the second round of the fours warmup, Harry has them row by sixes, full slide and feathering, rotating pairs on his command, not the coxswain's. In the launch, he remarks to me with a chuckle that they look just like they did at the end of the spring, rowing just the same way. He is no longer surprised by this, having seen it so often, but he still marvels at it. He tells a story about Joe Burk, his college coach at the University of Pennsylvania, his sculling coach thereafter, and his coaching mentor. In the 1960s Burk watched a twenty-five-year reunion crew on the water and pointed out that they rowed the way they used to, a demonstration of how technique in the sport had changed since the 1930s. Harry saw the same thing at his 1968 crew's reunion. That crew used to really slam the front end, he said, and they still did it decades later. Both individual technique, seen in these rowers today, and a crew's style, seen in those reunion rows, become deeply ingrained. Harry says it takes a crew about five minutes of rowing together again, and they settle into the old pattern.

He runs them through one of his frequent technical drills, still rowing by sixes: using only the inside hand for a while, then "hands together," with the outside hand placed right next to the inside, rather than in its normal spot at the end of the handle. This arrangement requires the upper body to twist around more than usual as a rower reaches out for the catch, and Harry likes how the rowers can feel the latissimus muscles, under the armpit, engage when they apply pressure.

Most of the time he talks to the bow-four rowers about their catches, the timing of the square, and the drop of the blade to the water. The four-seat isn't rotating his shoulders enough, and Harry tells him to watch his blade as he slides forward and puts it in the water. Often rowers fix their gaze on the torso in front of them, where they can see what rowers and blades are doing in peripheral vision. Asked to look out at their blade, they get uneasy, as if they think they will fall out of the boat. The four-seat obeys, though, and eventually that gets his outside shoulder rotating a little more.

About a mile and a half downstream, after turning toward the Boston University Bridge, they finally row all eight. They stop on the other side of the bridge for a short break and drink of water, and then head off again into the "Basin." The Massachusetts Avenue Bridge spans the wide river in the distance, and beyond it rises a hump of trees and buildings, Beacon Hill and downtown Boston, with the gleaming dome of the State House in full view. The Charles River Basin, to geographers, is the whole nine-mile stretch of river from the dam at Boston Harbor to the next dam upstream, in Watertown. But to Boston's rowing community, the Basin is just the stretch below the BU Bridge, where the river widens dramatically for a mile and a half, with MIT on the Cambridge side and the Back Bay neighborhood on the Boston side. It is divided into "upper" and "lower" sections by the "Mass. Ave. Bridge" (which is actually the Harvard Bridge, though no one calls it that). If you row from one end of the basin to the other, twenty-five hundred meters in a single effort, it is called a "basin piece" or a "basin shot." Harvard crews do a lot of basin shots, testing themselves against other Harvard crews.

As we come into the basin a wind hits us from the east, a headwind. "A sea breeze, it'll cool us off!" says Harry. There's a little chop on the water from the wind, but he says he can't resist taking them into the basin: "probably the last time we'll be all alone down here." As they approach Mass. Ave. he tells the coxswain, "last twenty and we'll stop." The cox counts twenty strokes and they weigh oars exactly under the bridge. As they spin the boat around, the cox asks whether to take the crew across the river to the Cambridge shore, which would be the normal traffic pattern. Harry says no, we'll go back on this side. "Looks like we have the river pretty much to ourselves."

On the way back to the boathouse they row briefly by fours and sixes again as Harry continues to talk about what the blade should be doing on the recovery, as it travels feathered above the water and then squares up and comes down for the catch. He wants the blade to be fully squared just as it stops moving toward the bow, and he wants the rowers to start applying pressure to the oar as soon as the bottom edge of the blade touches the water. He describes to the crew a drill in which blades scrape across the water for the whole recovery, even as they are squared and drawn into the water at the catch. "A long time ago," he says—"from your perspective, not mine—they used to row like that."

Comments to various members of the crew: "light touch in the hands"; "don't push the handle too much into the catch"; "rotate the handle in the fingers of the inside hand." He tells the bow seat his blade is staying in the air square for too long, how it should hit the water earlier. "Bow seat doesn't get the picture," he mutters to me in the launch. In about fifty minutes of coaching, he says nothing to the stern three.

Boat and oars back in their racks, the crew gathers in the boat bay. Harry says, "Alright—jumpsquats, back extensions, ten minutes on the erg, and we'll see you tomorrow."

A week later, it is pretty much the same story. Harry takes an eight out at 3:00 p.m. When the crew shoves off the dock he is typing an e-mail on the computer in the shop, and he keeps at it for a few minutes. He walks out to the dock just as they emerge from upstream, rowing by sixes; the engine is a little fussy again so he has to chase them down, and catches them just below the John Weeks footbridge, the second bridge from the boathouse, where they have stopped. He did not tell them to do that; the coxswain just knew she should wait. They continue by sixes for another mile downstream. "I just can't get over it, that we can come out here at three, and there's no one else on the river. It's too good to be true." And sure enough, a big powerboat approaches from the BU Bridge as they turn, leaving a sizeable wake behind.

Harry talks to the five-seat about his inside arm at the finish: He has been shrugging his inside shoulder, trying to draw the blade upwards. Harry tells him to keep the shoulder down, and think about the elbow moving backwards past his body, rather than upwards. They go off by fours, and Harry keeps talking to the five-man. "Good, that's the idea. It's going to feel like you're doing less work at the finish, for a while, but you don't mind that, right?" he says with a chuckle. They do a little with bow four, then a stretch with two sixes, all the while trailing the powerboat. It has slowed down by the time they head under Anderson Bridge and pass the boathouse, and a second one has appeared next to it. Harry has them go all eight. He tells the cox to stay to the right and go around the motorboats, and then sends them off alone at two-thirds power for three miles up to North Beacon Street, the farthest bridge upstream, and then home. "Careful rowing guys, steady with the bodies as you approach the catch, good length, good pry from the catch right to the finish."

Until now, all the other crews on the water have been from Harvard: Bill with the freshmen, Charley with an eight and a four, Linda with two lightweight freshman eights. At 3:45 Simmons College is just launching two crews from the Riverside Boat Club, two Riverside scullers are out, and a few recreational scullers from Weld criss-cross the river between Anderson and the Weeks footbridge. But still, the river traffic is light.

Harry turns and joins two coxed fours, just heading downstream in their warmup past Newell. One of them quickly gets the okay to go all four at two-thirds power, down the straight section of river known as "the Powerhouse Stretch," from Weeks to the turn above BU, while Harry keeps the other crew rowing by pairs the whole way down. "Keep the blade turning, squaring up all the way before it goes in," he tells the bow-man. "You tend to catch without it being all the way square." The two-man is told to "let the oar raise the hands for the catch." From the bottom, they head back upstream to the Weeks bridge at two-thirds, then do three more round-trips of the Powerhouse, the first minute of each stretch at two-thirds, the rest at three-quarters. It's not exactly the same workout that the eight is doing, but it's very close to the same total distance: roughly six miles of rowing from the end of the warmup. The fours are doing shorter segments at slightly higher intensity, which may help keep these smaller, more unstable boats moving well; plus, they are getting a break every four minutes or so as they spin around.

The pattern Harry sets out for these pieces is classic for him. Over and over during the year his crews will do building pieces, starting at one intensity and then increasing it later in the piece. Often, as the workout progresses, each piece will start at a higher intensity than the last one did: If the first pieces build from two-thirds to three-quarters, the next few might go from three-quarters to 90 percent, and the last one will end at full pressure. It's hard not to correlate this with their typical race profile: though frequently down off the start, they seem to get faster and faster as the race goes on.

On the way home, Harry's red baseball cap flies off in the wind and lands in the water behind the launch. He stops, backs up, fishes it out. "I have about a 50 percent record of retrieving them," he says. He guns the engine to catch up with the crews.

Devin Adair (Mahony) '86

I got to Harvard at the tail end of the era accurately dubbed "Harry, The Sphinx of the Charles." This was during the gestation phase of Kathy's influence on Harry's communication skills. A few years BEFORE her influence trickled down into his coaching style. So, during my era, we were still being coached by "The Man of Few Words."

Harry's communication style at the time had a strong influence on me, even before I got to Harvard.

I was recruited for crew by several colleges (there's no accounting for taste out there), and received my fair share of letters, phone calls, and visits from various college coaches my senior year in high school. Peter Washburn, my coach at the time, told me that Harry was interested in having me come to Harvard.

This would be something I had to take on faith, because . . . no word from Harry. No urging to apply early acceptance, no offers of no-show jobs turning on automatic sprinklers, no grand promises of being groomed to compete at the Olympic level. Seriously, just No Word.

Peter told me when we raced at the Head of the Charles that fall that Harry wanted to meet me. As you can imagine, I was both excited and awed at the prospect of meeting Harry Parker.

It went something like this:

My coach leads me over to Harry on the dock of Newell boathouse the Saturday morning of Head of the Charles.

"Harry, this is Devin Mahony."

Harry, looking preoccupied, with many shells dangerously close to colliding on the Harvard dock, turns to me for about two seconds. He delivers that inscrutable stare that drills into your core and says abruptly, "Nice to meet you."

Then, he turns his back and walks down the dock.

I had not uttered one word. That was the sum total of our conversation.

Fall turns into spring, and no word from Harry, but many calls and letters from every other coach. I say to Peter, "Are you SURE Harry wants to me go to Harvard? Are you SURE that he's going to let me cox on the men's team?" Peter's reply was always, "Yes."

I get my acceptance letters, and I got one from Harvard.

Peter, my coach, tells me that everyone wants to know what I'm going to do as soon as possible and that Harry also, is very interested in what I might do.

Of course, I'd done my research on every coach, on every rowing program at this point and the stats didn't lie. Harry was the best, most winning coach in the history of college athletics. Across any sport.

My grand plan, in perfectly predictable teenage form, was to get into Harvard then reject Harvard, since my entire family worshipped the school and matriculated there for generations. But then, there was the fact that I wanted to go fast, and I really, really wanted to win.

I got back to my dorm that afternoon, and received a phone call. This is back in the day when dorms had a phone on every floor that all the students shared. I walked down the hall and picked up the phone.

The conversation went something like this:

"Hello, this is Devin."

"Hello Devin. This is Harry Parker."

LONG PAUSE. I am floored. Struck speechless, in fact.

Harry says, "I'm calling to tell you congratulations on getting into Harvard."

"Thank you," I say.

"And I want you to know, if you decide to come here, you'll be welcome in my rowing program."

LONG PAUSE. Of deafening silence.

"Okay," I say.

"Well. Good-bye," Harry says.

And, then, he hung up.

That was the sum total of my experience of being recruited by Harry Parker.

Why did I decide to go to Harvard?

Because Harry didn't promise me anything. He simply let me know that if I wanted to step up and try to compete at his level, he would give me the chance. Nothing less and nothing more.

Which is actually part of the magic and the enduring excellence of his coaching style.

Harry entered my life when I needed more than anything to feel the steady influence and unrelenting challenge of a mentor who would carve out a set of non-negotiable standards.

The true magic of Harry's coaching style is that instead of fashioning himself as the Man to Be Looked Up To, in the ego gratifying way of many leaders, Harry steps out of the way of his athletes and holds up a map and a mirror to them—"Here are the goals that you might like to meet," he seems to say. "You decide whether you are made of the right stuff."

There is no greater gift to a person than to help them form their own personal standards. Circumstances change, and the cult of personality that can be created by one rowing program, or any other program by a charismatic coach, will not be replicated in a young athlete's life after graduation. We are all, no matter where we go, or what we set out to do, on our own.

CHAPTER 2—OCTOBER

Mother Newell

AUTUMN PASSES QUICKLY IN BOSTON AND ESPECIALLY AT HARVARD, where the academic term starts so late. Only a month after the team starts rowing together, the Head of the Charles is upon them.

October 16, Tuesday. The Head is this weekend, and already the boathouse is buzzing. The Dutch student club Nereus is borrowing Harvard equipment for the race and they are here in the early afternoon, some rigging the boat, the rest basking in the sun on the dock—it's just barely warm enough to do this. Another foreign duo arrives around three, finds Charley, and takes out the double scull they are borrowing for the race. Joe is busy clearing space for visiting scullers on the racks out on the dock. He moves six of the recreational sculling boats out to a trailer in the parking lot. "I'm already exhausted, and it's only the beginning of the week!" he says. Meanwhile Harry moves constantly, talking to the foreign crews, to Joe, to his rowers as they locate and rig their boats. The lineups for the Head are rowing today for the first time.

Harry's squad is big, enough for four eights with a few left over. The demographics are typical: Most started rowing at private high schools before coming to college, but there are a few in the mix who learned with Bill Manning in their freshman year. (It is three years since the last non-recruit made it into the varsity eight.) All of the varsity heavyweights are white, except for two coxswains—one black, one Asian. There are two Australians on the team and one each from Canada, Bulgaria, Serbia, Germany, England, and Ireland. There is a pair of identical twins, Harry's third set in seven years. The oarsmen are smart, gentlemanly, funny, friendly, and hardworking. Several members of the team are above six feet tall, and many cluster between 190 and 200 pounds, though some of the best technical rowers are a little bit smaller.

When Harry graduated from the University of Pennsylvania, he weighed 172 pounds and stood at exactly six feet. He had started rowing to fulfill the Navy ROTC physical education requirement, and though he was a lightweight his first year, the great sculler and Penn coach Joe Burk brought him over to the heavyweights thereafter. Harry wrote later that his childhood athletic attempts had been limited by a lack of skill, but that in rowing, he "found a sport that demanded some skill, granted, but placed a much higher premium on plain hard work and persistence." In 1955, Harry's sophomore year, the Penn varsity was a truly great crew, and Harry was in the two-seat, on the port side. In photos he is visibly smaller than the others in the boat. In one shot of the crew in practice, Harry is dwarfed by those around him, his body nearly eclipsed by the man in front, his shoulders lower, his head the only one that breaks the straight line of heads running from stroke to bow. His square jaw juts out, his mouth is slightly open for an aggressive exhale, and he is looking out at his blade. That crew beat Harvard and Navy in their annual race after a long losing streak, won the Eastern Sprints, then went to Henley and won the Grand Challenge Cup. Harry stayed with the heavyweights. Sometimes, these days, it seems he will give a little extra attention to the slightly smaller rower who has the drive to compete in a world of bigger men.

Today, Wayne Berger is at home with his sick daughter, so Harry has to look after all his crews alone. One eight rowed this morning, but this afternoon there are two more eights and two fours, and they will all launch at slightly different times. Harry will spend all afternoon on the water, following each crew for some stretch of river, then switching to another as they pass. The workout is a warmup downstream to Mass. Ave. and then back to BU, then a steady piece over the three-mile Head course at two-thirds pressure, and finally a few short bursts at racing speed on the way home. Harry has five crews entered: an eight full of seniors and another of sophomores, both in the Championship Eights event, and one entry each in the Club Eights, the Championship Fours, and the

Club Fours. Entries at the Head are not easy to come by, but Harry has managed to boat his entire squad this year.

The Club Eight, who launched upstream a few minutes ago, is now coming back down, so Harry leaves the bustling boathouse to join them on the water. A photographer from the *Harvard Crimson* is aboard, getting shots for the paper's Head of the Charles supplement. As Harry eases the launch out of its berth the sophomore eight is just putting their boat on the water, and he asks the coxswain if he knows the workout: Since they, too, will head upstream initially, they will be on their own for a while. The cox nods, but the doubt is evident on his face, and when Harry reminds him that it's all written on the bulletin board he runs off to check it. Coxswains run the workout in the absence of direct instructions from the coach, so they need to know what the plan is. Harry turns the launch and catches up with the Club Eight.

This crew is composed almost entirely of juniors, but not by design. It was put together after the Championship Four, the senior eight, and the sophomore eight, which is close to last year's first freshman boat, but not quite. The one sophomore in this otherwise-junior crew is a big, strong rower who nonetheless didn't make it into his own boat from last spring. He was beaten out by the Bulgarian, who spent last year in the second freshman eight, all the while working to improve himself. He came in almost every morning to train, and kept getting better over the summer. "He put in an amazing amount of time," says Harry. "And it paid off."

He follows the Club Eight as they warm up down to Mass. Ave. and turn. One of the rowers is a little short on the slide, slowing down too much into the catch. Harry tells him to "approach the stern with a little more abandon." The crew heads off on their run up the course. The sophomore eight passes Harry going downstream near the BU boathouse, but he doesn't see them in the glare of the sun. A four comes through the bridge right after, and Harry turns to follow.

This is the Championship Four, composed of returning members of last year's varsity, all seniors. This makes it the fastest four in the squad, or nearly so. Four years ago the four returning varsity rowers wanted to row together, and they finished second in the Head to the US national team four, only two-tenths of a second behind them. Harry kept boating the Champ Four entry this way very year, and they've had good success, finishing second or third every year. This four looks good, Harry thinks. Approaching Mass. Ave. he finally sees the sophomore eight, with the twins in the stern pair. He turns again, leaving the Champ Four on their own, and joins the sophomores as they head upstream for just under a mile, where the last crew of the day comes into view, the Club Four.

These rowers look uncomfortable and sluggish, the boat rocking back and forth at different points in the stroke. The port blades scrape the water on the recovery. Harry has them do twenty strokes at three-quarter power and then spin just before the BU Bridge. He has them row just stern pair, then just bow pair, coaching technique while the boat is more stable. Near Riverside Boat Club they stop and pick it up with the whole crew. "Let's get it right now." He tries to encourage them.

"These are three of the heaviest guys in the squad, and three of the lowest erg scores," Harry tells me. The stroke is a very good rower, having nearly made the varsity eight a couple of years ago, but he has been away from school for eighteen months. The three-seat was a very successful high school rower—his boarding school crew won the New England Interscholastics, a high standard—and his freshman crew at Harvard was good, but since then Harry's assessment is that "he doesn't really like to train": a good rower, boat-mover, and racer, but lacking the fitness built up from consistent training, especially over the crucial winter months (he drifted away from the team last winter, then showed up again in the spring). I ask if he hasn't been performing to his potential and Harry says, "well, who knows—maybe to his potential. But not to expectation."

"Light touch with the hands here." As he speaks into the megaphone, Harry's left hand leaves the steering wheel of the launch, reaches out slightly, the fingers wiggling as though tapping piano keys. "Just enough pressure to help keep the boat set. Careful rowing now on the way up, let's get it right." He repeats what he has been saying to the stroke (to keep the shoulders level in and out of the catch), starts putting the megaphone down, then brings it back up and briefly runs through the whole crew, giving each man a brief reminder: three-seat to rotate more on the way forward, two-seat to get more compression, bow to send the hands away before the knees start rising on the recovery. "That's good, let's have good focus now." The crew heads upstream on their own, still shaky but moving a bit better.

Harry drives in a slow circle in front of Newell, and the Champ Four emerges from the Anderson Bridge, just over halfway through their piece up the racecourse. He follows them for the last mile and a half to the finish line and then sends them back to Newell, assigned to do several ten-stroke pieces, from twenty-eight strokes per minute up to thirty-two or thirty-four, race cadence. Harry looks up and down this half-mile stretch of river, wondering where the Club Four is. "Before I pat myself on the back . . ." he says. "I sent four boats out, but I've only got three in so far." Finally they appear, having gone farther upstream than instructed. Instead of the tens that the other crews did, Harry talks them through a series of twenties, rating from twenty-four strokes per minute up to thirty-two. It's still rough; they have trouble reaching the ratings. The stroke is trying to force the stroke-rate, catching earlier than the other starboard rower. But the second twenty is better than the first, and as they round the bend below Eliot, they do a creditable piece at rate thirty.

The crew hugs the inside of the bend, and Harry brings the launch alongside, running close to the middle of the river. "If you want a crew to look fast, have them row close to the shore," he says. "If they're out there, you don't get nearly the same sense of speed." The notion reminds him of a trip in a fighter jet he took after high school, at a ROTC summer camp. When the pilot brought the plane closer to the ground, he suddenly got a sense of how fast they were going. He says it was one of the most amazing experiences of his life. The only disappointment was that they didn't have to parachute out.

—◦—

The Head of the Charles is known as "America's fall rowing festival," and sometimes "the Super Bowl of rowing." Over two days, thousands of rowers race up the river, three miles starting at the BU boathouse, passing under six bridges and around some sharp turns, with tens of thousands watching from the shore. For most rowers, this is the only time so many people will pay attention to what they are doing. Autumn leaves are turning color. The regatta organizers arrange music, food, a lively fair-like atmosphere along the riverbank. And since there are events for all levels of the sport, from Juniors to Senior Veterans, it has become by default a large-scale rowing reunion. At Newell, huge flags bearing the graduating years of the freshman and senior classes flutter from the two balconies over the dock. Harry plays host to the reunion as well as coach to his team and manager of the boathouse.

Boathouses tend to be removed from campus, and are so specialized and contained in use that the rest of the university is almost irrelevant. Apart from the occasional intramural crews using the tanks, the facilities are not shared in the way the basketball court and the swimming pool are shared. Almost everyone who comes to Newell is on the rowing team or closely tied to it; anyone else is a visitor. And if you visit, you should talk to Harry: He is in charge, as he has been for forty-five years.

If you want to borrow something, you ask Harry. If someone wants access to the dock, they talk to Harry. Harry knows where your boat's missing seat and riggers are. He knows if the engine for the new tank is working well. He knows if the paper towels in the bathroom need to be replaced. Harry controls who has keys to the front door, the side door, the office, the shop, and the lock on the gas pump. If you break something, you have to apologize to Harry.

Harry Parker and Newell Boathouse recall the classic pairings of an old man and his ship, or house, or car, or tool. They simply go together, their existences identified with one another unmistakably and irrevocably. If Harry's shoe catches a nail as he walks up the dock, he will go get a hammer and bang it in, then look around for any others; it's like he is looking after himself.

Newell Boathouse is clad in red slate shingles that fall off sometimes. When a whole load of shingles were needed for a repair project, a quarry in Scotland had to be re-opened to supply them. The roof, which has both wide gables and small dormers, is gray-green slate. The style has been called "Old English," and a writer once described Newell as "grim and grand as an 1890 railroad depot." There is a low, wide porch on the road side of the boathouse: roofed, dark, with pairs of thick crimson columns spaced across it. The porch adjoins the sidewalk and the parking lot, and since everyone enters and exits here it's called the "front door." When you open it you can look straight through a small vestibule, down the length of a boat bay, and out the bay door directly opposite, a rectangle filled with light and water. That other side, the dock side, is the real front of the boathouse. Here it spreads out toward the world it cares about. The four bay doors are big like barn doors; they slide open wide and the life of the boathouse flows out onto the expanse of the dock, toward a panorama of Cambridge, Boston, the river world.

When you carry a shell to the water, you walk out the bay doors and descend in four stages to the water: fifteen feet almost level, sixty feet down a real slope, fifteen more nearly level again, then a short drop to the actual floating dock, about ten feet wide. You carry the boat upside-down at shoulder height, point the bow upstream as you approach the water's edge, then heave it overhead, flip it over, and lower it gently. The dock at Newell extends upstream and downstream, beyond the width of the boathouse itself. It can launch or land three eights at a time, end-to-end, with room to spare. An eight is about sixty feet long, a bit shorter at the waterline than the *Santa Maria*. The several coaching launches are parked on an auxiliary dock and on the boathouse side of the floating dock. The boat bays are so full of boats that extra racks now adorn either side of the big slope of dock, holding some pairs, fours, and recreational singles. Newell has its own gas pump, tucked in the upper corner of the dock under the eaves.

In the boat bays, shells are stacked fifteen feet high on five layers of thick wooden beams. They gleam in ordered, linear repose. The bays are mostly places of stillness and quiet talking, with the occasional bustle of a crew appearing, lining up along their boat, and a coxswain shepherding them out to the river with ritualized calls. There are four boat bays, identical in size. Above them is a second floor: in the middle, an enormous room filled with rowing machines, weight equipment, spin bicycles, and a wrestling mat for stretching. The floors are narrow-planked, varnished wood. The space overhead is once again like a barn, with huge beams supporting the gabled roof, dark triangles in the dimness above, hung with banners from regattas won. The walls are covered with sacred memorabilia. Trophy oars, framed photos of champion crews, posters from regattas, the famous London *Evening News* poster from 1914, after a win at Henley: WELL ROWED HARVARD. Olympic champion Bryan Volpenhein, who did not go to Harvard, wrote in 2003 about his experience at the annual ergometer championships in Boston. He felt he always did better if he trained at Newell the day before. "There is something about that place," he said. "You can feel the ghosts of legends falling with the dust from the rafters. Maybe it's the dirt and sweat and time in the corners and cracks—it defines function over form . . . It feels rugged. It feels like rowing."

The upstairs layout is nearly symmetrical, but not quite. On either side of the central erg room are the team rooms: on one side, in a line, a big shower room, the varsity heavyweight locker room, and their lounge; and on the other side, in the equivalent space, locker rooms for heavy and light freshmen, and for the varsity lightweights, and their lounge. It is not an equal division of space. The frosh locker rooms, and the varsity lounges, are lined with the yearly crew photos, usually a few years out of date. Last year, twenty years' worth of Harry's team photos were hung.

On the shower side, facing the road, is a crowded little bathroom. In the matching space on the other side is the office where five coaches work. The door says COACHES' ROOM in faded red paint. The bathroom and the office each open to a stairwell. The stairs outside the bathroom are unadorned and wooden and lead directly to the boat bays past walls with peeling gray paint. The landing and stairs outside the coaches' office are carpeted in crimson, and lead from a small photo and tribute to Marshall Newell, class of 1894, the boathouse's namesake, past a collection of 1968 Olympic posters, to the outrageously large photo of the outrageously spirited 1974 "Rude and Smooth" crew. Tucked underneath the stairs is a small bathroom and locker room for the few women who use Newell.

On the upstream end of the boathouse is the room with the "Old Tanks," two troughs of water with a set of sliding seats and oars down the middle. Balancing it on the downstream end, with a garage door onto the dock, is the workshop. Two long workbenches, a wall of racks holding shells in varying states of repair, a computer, a small refrigerator and microwave, a sink, lockers and clothes racks with warm-weather gear for coaches and coxswains, cox-boxes plugged in to recharge, old oars, cross-country skis, a band-saw and table saw, bottles of glues and resins, hand-tools, power tools, cubbies full of spare boat parts, an old moped, rope and anchors and buoys, seat-cushions, megaphones, bicycles, nails and screws and hooks and pieces of wood. An old wooden Harvard oar, decorated as a gift for Harry ("coaching winners for 25 years") leans in a corner, twenty years out of date. Also in the shop you will often find Joe Shea. Joe is both a specialist in boat-building and repair, and a general handyman for the boathouse. He is not as crotchety as such boatmen often are. He has a sense of humor and an easy relationship with the rowers, who recognize and revere his ability to fix all problems mechanical, in or out of a boat, thoroughly and precisely. His job is in part to make sure the boathouse works the way Harry wants it to work, and he has figured that out well enough to operate comfortably and freely, even innovatively. When you try something new and tell Harry about it, he might nod and say something like, "okay, that's alright." He might do this even if it's not his jurisdiction; you might be talking about your new shoes, or an alteration of your bicycle. The ritual of seeking Harry's approval is ingrained, both in the supplicant and in Harry.

Over the weekend of the Head, alumni are everywhere: mostly on the dock, but also on the balconies, in the boat bays, in the shop checking live results, and upstairs. Dinko Vucemilovic '97 is in town for the weekend from New York City. He wanders the second floor, happy to find that the team photos from his era have finally been hung. Harvard oarsmen call the boathouse "Mother Newell." Vucemilovic says it is "more like home than home."

———

Before they row the Head of the Charles, Harry reminds his men of the racing attitude he expects. He tells them to be strong and persistent, to take the first couple of minutes to settle into it, focusing on length, power, and rhythm. Try to hold off chasing crews, he says, but if passed, stay strong and keep going. Your body can keep working hard for longer than you think. His rowers have trained to push themselves for long periods of time, and to push harder as time goes on, taking on whatever new challenge is posed, and that is the same strategy that Harry expects during a race. Anything more nuanced than that, any bursts to pass a crew, jumpstart the rhythm, or refocus the crew, will have to come from the rowers and coxswain in the boat. They are in charge of their own race.

Harry's Club Eight has bow number 6, and a crew of recent alumni has number 7, right behind them. The two crews collude on a cops-and-robbers costume theme: #6 wears striped shirts and masks, while #7 wears blue shirts, silver stars, and police hats. The robbers escape quickly from the cops, and win the event by fifteen seconds over Northeastern.

The Champ Four faces a tough field: The US national team enters the four that won the World Championships this year, as well as another crew of top national team oarsmen. Penn AC, a club from Philadelphia, has a four that includes three US team rowers. The two US boats finish first and second, four seconds apart in a sixteen-minute race. Penn AC and Harvard are third and fourth, also four seconds apart and about fifteen seconds behind the national team. The next fastest four is Stanford, nearly forty more seconds behind Harvard. It's a very strong showing. The seniors finish twelfth in the Champ Eight, the sophomores twenty-seventh. The seniors are tenth among the college crews, but most other schools have probably prioritized this boat, whereas Harry has spread out his top guys between the four and the three eights.

Many former Harvard oarsmen are on the dock over the weekend, and Harry greets them with pleasure, asks about their families, golf, bicycling. Baden Ireland '02 had an injured back during his last year at Harvard, and helped with the coaching. He introduces his fiancée. Harry asks about the back, and about his father. When Ireland mentions his father is sixty-five years old, Harry mishears it as "fifty-five," a rare sign of age in Harry. (On the water during the week, he asked the Champ Four how they liked the boat they were using, and when the stroke replied, Harry couldn't hear them. When the rower answered again, Harry put the speaking end of the megaphone to his ear—using the megaphone in reverse, a useful feature that the electronic megaphone can't replace—but he still couldn't hear. He shook his head, frowned, and waved his hand back and forth in resigned frustration.) Though it's true his face has wrinkles, and his hair has largely gone missing, Harry never acts "old." He seems younger than some of his former rowers.

Two of the most well-known ex-Harvard scullers, Tiff Wood and Gregg Stone, both from the class of 1974, have rowed a double together at the Head for decades. Stone sculls from Newell almost daily, but Wood now lives in Oregon and comes back for this weekend every year. They are now in the Senior Masters age group, and they usually finish in the top few places. This year they are fifth. Another crew largely composed of alumni is entered as Team Attager in the Senior Masters Eights, so they must average at least fifty years old. To make the average, some are older and some considerably younger. The stroke is Charlie Hamlin '70, former head of the Friends of Harvard Crew. They win the event by thirty seconds.

Adam Holland '94 is rowing in a Masters event for the first time at age thirty-four. Holland spent many years representing the United States in the coxless pair, with several different partners and usually coached by Charley Butt, the Harvard lightweight coach. In 2004 he nearly won the Olympic Trials in the single scull, after three years with no coaching at all. Today, when his wife and daughters greet him on the dock after the Masters Singles, the results show him winning by thirteen seconds. Later it turns out he has been beaten by three seconds, but for a while he is exultant.

Also sculling out of Newell today is Canadian Malcolm Howard '05, one of the keystones of the last Harvard heavyweight crew to win the National Championship. He has rowed for the Canadian team ever since, and has just anchored the eight that won the World Championships. Today he wins the Championship Single at the Head, just edging out the reigning world champion single sculler. One of Harry's guys comments, "so basically he's the best rower in the world right now." (A year later, Howard will win a gold medal in the eight at the Beijing Olympics.)

Harry himself does not race in the Head this year, due to an injured shoulder. It has recovered enough for him to row, in fact, but he hasn't had time to *train* for the Head, and he says it wouldn't be any fun to race in that condition. He hasn't won the Head in a long time, but he always manages to medal in his event, which is now the Senior Veteran Singles. The first time he rowed in the Head was in 1973, when there were no age categories. He recalls finishing fourth or fifth—"and I thought that was pretty good."

That was the first rowing event he had trained for since the 1960 Olympic Games, where he also finished fifth. Later that year, when Harry took the job as a rowing coach at Harvard, his competitive career was over, because the sport's rules of amateurism excluded paid athletes from competition, and the governing body classified coaches as "athletes." Under urging from rower-turned-coach Larry Gluckman, recalls Harry, the rowing community realized that the rule was "stupid." At the national rowing convention in 1973, in the middle of a conversation with Gluckman, Harry suddenly realized, "Ah! I can row in the Head of the Charles!" And that, he says, is when he started training again. To be sure, for the previous decade he had not been idle: He biked to and from his home in Winchester, sculled sometimes in the fall, ran the stadium, and rowed in the tanks with his athletes, sometimes "pretty hard."

Though Harry Parker raced in 1973, "Harry Parker" was not entered. Because of an injury, Harry had worried he would have to scratch come race day, and didn't like the idea of people speculating about why. So he entered as "T. Lazarus." The name "Lazarus" was a phony name often used by coaches on their "boating boards." These were wooden boards with columns of slots where paper slips bearing rowers' names could be inserted to arrange, and rearrange, crew lineups. Charley Butt still uses one at his desk. If a coach didn't have enough rowers available to fill out the eight seats in a boat, he might slide in one of the phony name slips, and "Lazarus" was one of them. (What about the initial "T"? "I added that. I have no idea why.") Harry thought it would be an amusing inside joke to enter as "Lazarus," though surely he appreciated the biblical allusion, the idea of reviving his rowing career, and he enjoyed everyone's surprise at seeing him race that day.

And the pattern continued. Harry says he "realized that I only train hard for an *event*, when there's a challenge ahead. Otherwise I exercise sporadically." So he sculls before the Head, and would bike harder in the spring those years before the Mount Washington climb. One spring day several years ago while coaching, he spied one of his annual opponents sculling past, yelled out through the megaphone, "You're cheating!" and then explained with a chuckle, "He's training out of season." Years after the automobile fumes deterred him from commuting by bicycle, he got back on the bike when some of his 1970s oarsmen, in particular Dick Cashin '75, invited him to join their annual fall ride through Vermont and New Hampshire. A few years later another group of alums were doing a long ride around Mount Rainier, and Harry took the place of one of them who had pulled out. That was the first time he trained really hard on the bike.

Harry's personal competitiveness is well known. The classic stories include elbowing his own oarsmen aside while running the Harvard stadium, hiding his frostbitten ears from the safety officials during a ski race, and deliberately avoiding hockey because he didn't think it was wise for him to wield a stick. Those who bike with Harry still see this drive. If you try to go faster than Harry, he will try to run you off the road. He would ask Dave Wagener '76, a frequent cycling partner with friends in the professional cycling world, about the latest gadgets and training techniques. (On the other hand, he sticks with his old Nishiki bike, rather than some flashy new model. When someone told him his handlebars were the wrong width, he told them no, they were exactly what he wanted.) Watching him race in the Head of the Charles recently, one Harvard alum said simply that Harry has "still got it." Another was surprised by the size of his biceps, and yet another struck by his visible determination. After the Mount Washington race one year, it took Wagener several rounds of questioning to get the results out of Harry, who kept saying his time was "not good" and wouldn't say how he placed in the over-sixty-five age group. "Why does that matter?" said Harry. "Because you're over sixty-five," said Wagener. It turned out Harry had won, and set a new record time. Seven years later, the record still stands.

That same year, Wagener and some classmates were planning to do some rowing with the Harvard squad, and wondered how fast their erg scores should be. Given that they were nearly fifty years old, Wagener thought seven minutes for two thousand meters was a good score, but Harry said he didn't consider them "old" and told Wagener they should be comparing themselves to his JV oarsmen. "Call me when you're under 6:30," he said.

Monday after the Head is an off day, but Tuesday is practice as usual. Except that Tuesday is blustery: Ripples from the wind sweep and swirl on the water in front of Newell, and there are rumors of gusts up to 30 mph. The paper on the bulletin board says "Warmup: 5' CII, 3 x 20. OTW: TBA. Post: TBA." Harry comes into the lounge where the 2:30 group is stretching, and offers them a choice. They could make their way carefully upstream, and hope to find good water above the Arsenal Street Bridge, or they could do a "triathlon-style" workout: erg, run, and a circuit of the stadium steps. He points out that the triathlon workout will be more time-efficient. There is one vote for rowing, and one rower doesn't have sneakers, so would like to erg the whole time. ("You don't keep sneakers here?" asks Harry. "You have to do that.") So it's decided: They go back out to the ergs. Five minutes later Harry has changed into a unisuit and he, too, sits down to row.

Over the Head weekend, Harry had answered an alumnus's query about the strength of the squad by saying that they would know more after the regatta. Later he admits that "it's hard to say" what he has learned about his squad relative to other colleges. Though he doesn't like how the Championship Eight event has become a race between the top varsity crews, he does think it is a good indicator of how strong the various schools will be next spring. So he learns something about their relative strengths. But since he hasn't prioritized his crews in the same way, the other teams haven't learned much about Harvard. Harry seems satisfied with that.

You get the sense he doesn't really need the comparison to know what his guys need to do this year. But his boating system wasn't a deliberate ploy to starve other coaches of information about his squad (at least, not entirely). It was because of the rowers themselves, and their desire a few years ago to row the four. Meanwhile, the reassembly of the previous year's freshman eight to race the Head as sophomores is a longstanding pattern, and Harry often boats "senior" eights for fall head races. Rather than creating a premature "first boat" only a few weeks into the year, this system keeps the tone a bit more lighthearted in the squad. Of course, all crews are expected to race as well as possible, and reap the rewards. Harry hadn't put the Club Eight in their event with an eye to winning, or even expected them to be in the running. They raced well, and it turned out to be good enough.

October 29. A week after the Head of the Charles, on a Monday afternoon, the team has a five-kilometer erg test. For a few, it's the first they have done this fall. The 2:30 group warm up on the ergs on their own, then stretch in the lounge, and start drifting back to the front row of machines around 2:45. Harry comes out and hovers at the front of the row, urging them to get going. He is a little impatient with the time they spend setting up the stereo to the right song or CD. He shakes his head with some disbelief. "Let's get going." As they sit waiting to start, setting up the computer monitors and taking their last-minute deep breaths, he talks gently, suggesting they aim for the pace of their previous test, then push it harder for the last one and a half kilometers.

Finally, all are sitting ready to go. Harry nods to the coxswain, who says, "ready all—row!" They explode from the catch, everyone rowing at essentially maximum effort for five to ten strokes. Twenty seconds in, most have settled to around twenty-six or twenty-eight strokes per minute, and are at the pace they intend to hold for the entire piece. "Good rhythm," calls Harry. This is a relatively strong subset of the squad, and half of them are holding five-hundred-meter splits of 1:40 or better, including the smallest one here, a senior from Ireland who is exactly the size Harry was in college. Harry wanders back and forth behind the row of ergs, looking at their splits, comparing to his list of what they did on their last test, and occasionally giving some encouragement. The coxswains, who in the boat talk constantly to the rowers, providing motivation and technical comments, do surprisingly little during an erg test; often they simply wait until the end and write down the scores. Harry has made no decrees on this point, however. If there are eight rowers testing, there are eight different dramas going on, and it's too much for a coxswain to direct at once. The cheering is mostly left to other rowers, who crowd behind their friends in vocal support.

Rowing with 1:40 splits, each kilometer takes 3:20, and the full 5k takes sixteen minutes and forty seconds. Every second on the split alters your final time by ten seconds. The 5k test is longer than the Head of the Charles, but shorter than the Harvard-Yale Race. Harry drifts away for a few minutes, but is back watching closely again when the rowers are in their final four minutes of rowing. "Good rhythm," he reminds them. "Be efficient. Stay strong now!" He claps his hands, tells each rower they're doing well. "Good persistence," he urges the group. At the end of the row of ergs, next to the small Irishman, a larger sophomore is struggling. His splits, which had averaged 1:41 for the first half, are drifting upwards—1:42, 1:43—and his stroke-rate is erratic. "1:42," Harry tells him. "Don't go below that." Others enter the last twenty or thirty strokes of the piece and start sprinting, increasing the power and rate, emptying their energy reserves. Each rower has to learn to pace himself, to know how much he can sacrifice early in the piece, how much fatigue and pain he can endure for those long minutes in the middle, and how early he can afford to start his sprint and not "die," losing all ability to pull and fading off disastrously at the end. Many of the rowers have dropped their splits by five or more seconds for these last two or three hundred meters. The big sophomore on the end tries to hold his 1:42s, but still some 1:43s creep in. He has more than a hundred meters still to row when the others have all finished. He manages a small spurt in the last few strokes. Harry stands next to him, talking him through these last seconds.

Each rower reacts differently to finishing an erg test. None of this group vomits, but it is not uncommon. Some slump forward over their ergs unmoving, some unstrap their feet and ease onto the ground, chests heaving. Some keep rowing lightly ("paddling"), warming down gradually while catching their breath. Some stand right up and get a drink of water. Harry claps again. "Well done! Good job, good improvement!"

When Harry takes an eight for a cool-down row after the erg test, two visiting high school seniors are in the launch, one of whom lives near Harry's hometown in Connecticut. He asks her if she knows the road from East Hartford to Glastonbury where the Pratt and Whitney air base is located. Harry, and his brothers before him, used to work at Augie and Ray's, a classic hot-dog stand near the base. It turns out her father grew up next door and used to work there too, and at this Harry lights up. He says they did good business during World War II, since the base workers came at shift changes and lunch breaks. "They had good hot dogs, too." Harry's older brothers were named Tom and Dick. Harry was supposed to have a different name, after his cousin, but when the cousin died his mother thought it a bad omen, and he became Harry "by default."

This young woman is surprisingly at ease with Harry. She is curious about some aspects of the rowers' technique, almost to the point of questioning it. Two of them hold their oars with their hands quite close together. Another makes a loud, sharp exhale at the finish of each stroke, audible from afar. She asks if they have been taught to row this way. Harry smiles a little and says no to both, and it's almost as though he hasn't noticed these things. "He's not the worst," he says of the noise-maker. "It's not a bad thing, though," he adds, explaining that the forcible exhale tends to evacuate the lungs more fully, and allow a deeper inhale right after. And the grip? "We don't really say much about it," he says. "We let them do what's comfortable."

Dan Grout '88

Harry was the master of understatement. I have somewhere the handwritten recruiting letter from Harry I got in high school in 1982, to the effect that Harvard is an academically well-regarded institution with a respectable rowing program and Boston is a nice place to go to college—as if Harvard were some midwestern start-up I had never heard of! Three pages as I recall.

We came from behind to pass Washington and then Princeton in the last five hundred to win the 1985 National Championship at Cincinnati. After we put Harry on shoulders and ran him into the lake he stood up and said, "Alright, good work, let's paddle out of here." As if we had just accomplished loading the boat trailer.

The only time I recall Harry betraying emotion during a practice was fall of '86 during a long intra-squad head race we called a "Tour de Charles." Four more or less even eights, seventy-five minutes or so, and we would spin the boats around once or twice during the piece. I was stroke and Lionel Leventhal was cox and we made an aggressive move to cut off another boat in front of Newell. Harry just lost it and banged on his launch and bellowed at Lionel so hard veins were bulging and spit flying: "LIONEL!!! LIONEL!!! HOW MANY TIMES DO I HAVE TO SAY IT??? SAFETY FIRST! SAFETY!!! FIRST!!!" He was furious. It should have been devastating for poor Lionel. But as soon as Harry stopped yelling, Lionel without missing a beat leaned forward with a gleam in his eye as we powered back up and said into his microphone, quietly but with a bite to his voice, "Okay, speed first safety last! Let's go!" Race on.

Joe Harvey '89

An erg piece that I remember from junior year: We were warming up in the new tanks and coming upstairs in pairs to do the test. I was rowing seven-seat that day, and the stroke (Dan Grout) and I came upstairs and finished warming up on the gamut. Then Dan let Harry know that he was injured or not fully back from an injury—suddenly Dan was out. I expected that Harry would bring up another port for me to row alongside; instead, he just said some version of, "Joe, you'll row the piece on your own." I had a flash of surprise and then worry, but it was time to start, so that's what I did. It turned out to be a great piece—one of the turning points for me that year, when suddenly I realized that I was stronger than I had been—and I remember knowing that it was going to be a good effort just a minute or two in.

With a few minutes to go, I remember Harry shouting out, "All right, Joe!" in that tone he had of celebrating and encouraging at the same time. He knew I had a good piece going, and I remember feeling that encouragement and acknowledgement of something special happening as fuel for the rest of the way. Looking back, I don't believe anyone else was there to witness it—but it was one of those quiet moments that continues to resonate today when I think of Harry.

CHAPTER 3—NOVEMBER

Steady at the Catch

THE DAILY—AND SOMETIMES TWICE DAILY—TRIP UP THE STAIRS AT Newell Boathouse takes a Harvard rower past several posters from the "Juegos de la XIX Olympiada" in Mexico City. Individually they are not remarkable (one depicts a cartoonish busload of athletes arriving at a large building, welcomed by a man saying, "Esta es su casa") but they were collected by Harvard men at the Olympic Games. If you are a Harvard man then maybe you, too, could someday go to the Games.

1968 had been the first time a Harvard eight had won the Olympic Trials, and it was also the last time the Olympic eight would be decided this way, by a simple open trial. Four years later the first "national team" program was set up, gathering from around the country the best individuals and creating crews out of that mix. Harry was in charge, and at the Munich Olympics in 1972 the eight won silver. Six out of that crew were from Harvard.

Since then, many Olympic hopefuls have trained out of Newell: often Harvard grads, but not always. Harry, Charley, Bill, and Linda have all taken crews to world competition at various levels. (Harry's last US crew, after twenty-five years of coaching national teams on and off, men and women, sweep and sculling, was the 1990 men's coxed four. He realized, he says, that he prefers coaching Harvard.) Recent elite crews at the boathouse have been the women's single, the men's pair and double, the lightweight men's single, and the lightweight men's double. The custom is that these guest rowers use the freshman heavyweight locker room: There is usually some free locker space, and Bill likes his athletes to see what they can aspire to. Adam Holland has been training at Newell for nearly twenty years. He was on the cover of *Newsweek* in 1996, in the moments before his Olympic pairs race, bowing his head in honor of the Atlanta bombing victims. His last time on the US team was the 1999 World Championships in Canada, but he made several attempts afterward, sometimes coming heart-breakingly close, and he can still be found at the boathouse rowing his single. The boat is named "Sisyphe Heureux"— Holland is the sort of man who puts a quotation from Camus on his boat. A few years ago Harry bought Holland's pair for the use of the Harvard team, and naturally it was christened in his honor. The name on the bow reads "J. Adam 'Furioso' Holland '94."

Holland's locker is in the far corner of the freshman locker room. The room has two banks of locked cubbies on opposite walls, and open locker spaces with hangers for rowing gear, under a high shelf. The wall above that shelf is hung with photographs of Harvard freshman crews—mostly the first boats, but also some especially successful second boats. Holland's water bottle sits on the shelf above his hanging clothes, where the eaves angle down toward the outer wall of the boathouse. There is space in this corner of wall for a single photograph, and it's the oldest one in the room: the 1961 freshman crew. The water bottle and a pair of shoes obscure it. In the picture, to the right of the crew in their racing gear, stands Harry Parker. His hair is short and tidy so his ears stick out prominently, and he wears a white sweatshirt with crossed oars and HARVARD arched over the top. It looks a lot like the ones he hands out to the varsity letter-winners at the end of every year. In later team pictures, hung on the walls of the varsity lounge, Harry is more likely to be wearing a plaid shirt or a light jacket, and in many of them his left hand reaches across and holds his right wrist. He doesn't look out of place, but he doesn't look conspicuously like a coach, either. He could be a farmer, or a mechanic, or someone's father (which indeed he was, with sons George and David born in 1960 and 1963). His hair starts to recede in the 70s; by the mid-80s it is essentially gone. In 1989 wrinkles suddenly appear at the edges of his smiling face. Back in 1961 Harry is smiling only a little, and he looks very young—twenty-six years old, with neatly combed hair and no idea what is to come. His crew stands in two rows, but in front is a small man kneeling on the ground. The label says WASHBURN.

Ted Washburn '64 was the coxswain of the first crew Harry coached at Harvard. In 1963, when Harvey Love died mid-season and Harry took over the varsity, Washburn was the coxswain, and again in 1964 when they went undefeated. After graduating, Washburn became the coach of the Harvard freshmen, and he stayed on for twenty-four years. Eight of his crews were undefeated, and nine won the Eastern Sprints. They lost to Yale only four times.

The 1964 Harvard eight that Washburn coxed did not win the Olympic Trials, although that had been a major focal point for the team. Harry had just rowed the single scull in the 1960 Olympics in Rome, and he recalls that with that experience fresh in his memory, "right away the Olympics were the focus of my attention." He encouraged the athletes to aim for the trials as 1964 came closer. Contended by college crews and a few clubs, races were held first for the eight, and then some weeks later for the smaller boats, so there were second chances for those who had lost. After Philadelphia's Vesper Boat Club beat Harvard at the trials, the *Boston Globe*'s John Ahern described Harry as "on the verge of tears." As a consolation, four of them plus Washburn won the coxed four trial and finished seventh at the Tokyo Games.

And then, back at Harvard, the Olympic hunt started again. In those days everyone was a walk-on for the rowing team. A few might have rowed at their prep school, but that was not the assumption. Harry's focus, and Washburn's, was to find extremely good athletes on campus, and teach them to row. Washburn was energetic and determined in this; it was like a game for him, and he considered anyone fair game, even those who had come to Harvard specifically to play other sports. He would browbeat, call them repeatedly, stay "on them like a rug," he recalls. He talked about the Olympics. Since college rowing was such a level playing field of inexperience, good athletes could progress quickly and become world-class within a single Olympic cycle. Washburn found basketball, squash, and football All-Americans, and brought them to Newell. He would challenge himself: "Can I get the center of the freshman basketball team to row?" Washburn convinced the number-one lacrosse player from the state of Maryland to switch to rowing, and he wound up as the stroke of the first freshman boat. Unsurprisingly this annoyed some other coaches at Harvard, who were losing their star players. Harry went along with Washburn's game (though he did call him off from pursuing the son of a famous Dallas Cowboys player), but in the 70s and 80s, when there were scholarships involved, Washburn says it was no longer funny to poach in the same way. And by then, everything had changed.

Ted Washburn's counterpart at the University of Pennsylvania, Ted Nash, "introduced real recruiting to the sport of rowing. And he was very, very good at it." Nash would send the kids cards at holidays, visit their homes, and send letters to their parents, says Washburn, to convince them to come to Penn. And apparently he had some sway in the admissions office. A Harvard alum from the 1970s recalls that Nash might give a recruit a Penn application with a red star stuck to the front. A classmate of his got the red-star application but passed it on to a friend, a non-rower. The friend got into Penn.

Washburn says that in the face of Ted Nash's recruiting style, "Harry was speechless with indignation," and that he too was angry. They both had a "strong emotional attachment" to the traditional style of building a team: find the good athletes, put them all out in the barge, and teach them to row. Until the 1970s, the Harvard coaches felt recruiting from high schools was unnecessary—they had just gone to the Olympics, after all. Plus, says Washburn, "Harry has his own set of ethics," and he fundamentally disapproved of approaching athletes himself. Harry is "not a salesman." Harry himself says he preferred that his athletes were there "because they wanted to come to Harvard, not just to row, and also that they were truly representative of the student body . . . And you know, lots of other people felt the same way. There were lots of excesses involved with recruiting, undue pressure on the kids, and so it was not easy to go that route." And so, Washburn remembers Harry's early efforts as "very mild": He would call high school coaches and simply ask if they had anyone on their team who was interested in Harvard. He never spoke with the kids himself, and never pushed them to come. "In the best of all worlds you wouldn't do intensive recruiting," says Harry.

But soon everyone was following Penn's lead, and "it became clear that you were not going to remain competitive" if you didn't make more of an effort. By the mid-70s Washburn had a significant number of experienced rowers in his freshman squad, maybe half. Al Shealy, legendary stroke of the "Rude and Smooth" crews in 1974 and 1975, was one of the early pre-recruits. Washburn says the watershed year was 1980, when he had twenty-four experienced freshmen and fielded four freshman eights that lost to no one. Despite his early aversion to recruiting, Harry eventually embraced it. "Recruiting changed for Harry when it became a competitive sport," says Washburn. "Now it's a board game for him." And that allows him to pursue it fervently, as long as everyone plays by the rules.

⚓

When Harry told the recruit in October that he lets the oarsmen "do what's comfortable," it was more than just an idle comment. That approach is one of the hallmarks of Harry's coaching over the years. He does not impose a particular "style" of rowing, though he makes sure the rowing is effective. He doesn't tell the rowers exactly how far forward their bodies should tilt before they start the slide, or when they should start swinging them back during the drive, or what layback angle they should have at the finish, or what the precise ratio of drive and recovery times should be. None of those things is consistent from one crew to the next, or even within a single crew. When asked if there is anything that unifies Harry's crews from year to year, Liz O'Leary, the Radcliffe coach who has watched them for more than two decades, replies, "not unless you look at the blades."

Harry coaches the blade: "It's the working end," he says matter-of-factly. It is the blade's action on the water that moves the boat, so everything about the rowing stroke is directed toward effective use of the blade: It must enter and exit the water cleanly, and in between it must be buried and pushing against the water. His oarsmen "could be doing the worst things" with their bodies, Harry laughs, but as long as the blade looks good, he might not notice anything else. Some coaches carefully analyze body movements and try to create a specific, uniform look throughout the crew. But Harry looks at the blade, and everything follows from that. If you look at a photo of a Harvard heavyweight crew, the men may look ragtag, rough, wild, or awkward. But if you had a film of their blades, they would glide smoothly together at the same height toward the catch, square up smoothly, and drop sweetly into the water.

Harry seems to look at catches more than finishes, and he looks at the blade in the water, but not so much the swirling "puddle" it leaves behind (the size and quality of puddles are a much-discussed topic among rowers). But it is not that Harry talks only of blades: He will correct an oarsman's use of fingers, hands, arms, shoulders, or anything else, but it seems always related to what he has seen the blade doing. And he will do this very quickly. He will turn his head to look at a crew and, with only a second's delay, raise the megaphone and give a detailed set of instructions for one rower's inside arm, or outside shoulder, or last two inches of slide on the recovery. Ted Washburn, who has coached nearly as long as Harry, agrees that Harry "has a good eye."

He has a good eye, he knows what he wants to see, and he knows what to tell the athlete so that they can produce it. And, crucially, he is *right* about his vision of effective rowing. Right enough of the time that his athletes are successful.

Dave Reischman, the Syracuse coach, who worked with Harry several years ago and has remained close to him ever since, recalls a subtle comment from Harry. He wasn't necessarily aiming for the "best" rowing stroke possible, he said. He had figured out a certain version of good rowing technique that he, Harry, could convey to college students in a way that they could learn to do it.

At the 1978 convention of the National Association of Amateur Oarsmen, Harry gave a technique workshop and demonstration. A paraphrased transcript depicts an unusually verbose Harry Parker, breaking down the rowing stroke into four phases: propulsion, release, recovery, catch. His rowers might get a similar speech (once!) during a training year, with Harry demonstrating in the tanks or on the erg, with the focus almost exclusively on catch and propulsion.

There are few surprises in Harry's presentation, though there is a noticeable deviation from the familiar description of the stroke sequence and how the rowing muscles should engage. From the crouching position at the catch, with arms reaching out in front, the usual sequence is: legs pushing, back opening, arms pulling. Most coaches tell their athletes that, for the first part of the stroke, the arms should stay extended "like ropes," merely holding the connection between the oar handle and the big latissimus dorsi muscles that connect the armpits to the middle of the back. A few years ago some rowers were watching a video at Newell of the world sculling finals, and they criticized one woman for her habit of grabbing the water early with bent arms, then holding that slight bend until the final pull at the end of the drive. Harry, watching from the back, said simply, "no, you can do that." If you look at film of Harry rowing his single scull fifty years ago, you will see that initial arm grab. And in his 1978 workshop he explicitly says that "all three major muscle groups used in rowing must be engaged" at the catch. "The idea is to bend a little as you put the blade in the water, so that the elbow moves back slightly and helps to draw the blade against the water." At least one of his current squad does this. Harry does not explicitly teach it now, but he allows it.

What emerges in Harry's talk is the theme of avoiding orthodoxy, of principles taking precedence over rigid form. Don't be strict about the recovery sequence of arms, body, legs—make it natural. Don't insist that the handle "must always come to the bottom of the ribcage," since people are "built differently." Don't worry about a breathing pattern—the body will figure it out. "Individuals vary considerably in their ability to do the things I've described . . . It is up to each coach to decide how we can best get the oarsmen to make these things happen. Some approaches work more effectively on some than on others, but if you do it well enough, they will learn to row hard, and that is most important."

Bill Manning finds it amusing when visitors come to Newell and ask him, "How does Harvard row?" There is no real answer. There is no "Harvard style."

Harry, says Bill, is good at separating effectiveness from style. He sees that there are different ways to be effective, and so doesn't push a particular style. He lets each man row hard in a way that works for him, as long as they are being effective in moving the boat. Bill has adopted this approach, realizing that his recruited rowers are too far along to be completely re-molded to any style he might have in mind. This year he ends up with an American and an Englishman in adjacent seats in the middle of his first eight, rowing about as differently as you could imagine. But it works, and they are fast.

There may be no real Harvard style, but there are tendencies. They typically reach far forward ("Harry's crews are *long*," says Liz O'Leary) sometimes to the point of having a "hunch" of the shoulders. They carry their blades close to the water on the recovery with a late, smooth square. Harry spends a lot of time drilling the catch, and the result is perhaps the most distinctive aspect of his crews' rowing: The drop of the blade into the water is quick, and yet somehow languid.

Also unlike many coaches, Harry does not mandate a particular rhythm. He will tell his athletes to change their individual motions to blend with those around them, but he will not tell the crew as a whole what their rhythm should be. Crucially, everyone must work with the rhythm laid down by the stroke seat, the one rower who cannot see any others. When you find someone who has their own good internal rhythm, "you go along with that," says Harry.

Ted Washburn, who works now with recorded voices, talks in acoustic metaphors. A voice is a conglomeration of signals with different frequencies, different wave forms. In a mellifluous voice, the waves coalesce. Washburn sees Harry as "tuning the boat to the stroke," so that the boat has "not eight wave forms, but one." If you can do this, he says, it is like magic: The motion becomes effortless, all eight bodies move together. It is rare, and "absolutely intimidating."

The rhythm comes from the rowers, so it can change as the rowers change. Harry: "A particular crew begins to move in a certain direction and you say 'oh, that's good, we'll do that.' So you *allow* it to happen." He did impose some changes in the mid-1960s, and then they "started moving too far in one direction. In '67–'68 we started rowing with a really hard catch, and it got to be a bit too far in '69–'70 so we backed off a little bit. And then when the Shealy crews came up in '73, '4, '5, we actually modified to fit the way he rowed, initially. He had a very good rhythm." Parker has found that this is what works for him: The crew ends up rowing the way the stroke rows.

Picking a stroke, then, seems of first importance, but how do you find one? "You stumble on it." Harry tries different strokes out during the first few months. By the end of the fall, it is fairly clear who the likely strokes are in the squad. Part of the tricky process of boating crews in the spring is making sure each crew has a decent stroke. Rhythm is not the same as technical form, and Harry has often found strokes who row very differently than everyone else but "get away with it, because they set a good rhythm." Graham O'Donoghue '02 was the stroke of the JV, and then filled in for the freshmen at Henley when their stroke became sick before the final. "You would not recognize him as a Harvard oarsman, the way he rowed. But he set a rhythm that people could follow. And he wasn't a particularly strong oarsman, but he set a rhythm that really worked . . . He won two races at Henley. We were utterly startled that the boat went as well as it did with him at stroke." Kip McDaniel '04, "not a particularly good example of Harvard rowing," is a fantastic stroke, routinely heading up crews full of much taller and stronger oarsmen and beating the competition. (The same may apply to the bow seat: Wayne Pommen '02, a three-year varsity bow-man for Harry, didn't row the way everyone else did, but was "extremely effective." He went on to row for Cambridge and for Canada. Why was Pommen never tried at stroke? "That's a good question. He was always a bow-man." Harry says this last with a tone that suggests "being a bow-man" is a matter of personal identity, not just rowing qualities.)

Though Harry will indeed give detailed instructions for body parts as small as the fingers ("apply pressure under the knuckles of your outside hand," he says to a rower who needs to improve the feathering of his blade), most of his oarsmen remember his coaching as being pared down to the basics. He "erred on the side of simplicity," according to Scott Henderson '95. One summary of Harry's technical coaching: "get the blade in and out at the same time, and pull as hard as you possibly can."

A favorite expression is "steady at the catch." The catch sequence is perhaps the most difficult component of rowing technique: The rower must bring the blade down into the water by raising his handle, and simultaneously change the direction his whole body is moving by pushing off his feet. Feeling and reproducing the correct timing of the blade drop and the direction-change is crucial, and Harry wants that last part of the forward slide, and the first part of the drive, to be under control. No "rushing" in the last quarter of the recovery, no sudden lurching with the back and shoulders. Controlled. Steady. It may come out as wordy as, "really hold the compression at the catch, bodies steady, feel the pressure on the blade as you start to push," but usually it is just "steady at the catch." The phrase is spoken so frequently the five syllables can be reduced to three, a quick preamble to some other more detailed instruction for an athlete. Harry's rowers hear it so often they might come away thinking it was all he ever said to them.

Memories of Harry's coaching fit well with Ted Washburn's acoustical tuning analogy: "little adjustments, day by day," accomplished with "short, sharp, occasional directives to individuals who were straying too far from his image of a good stroke." In between these directives Harry offers "lots of time for guys to just row, trusting in their athleticism to find the right movements." Recalling the theme of the 1978 technique workshop: Harry insists on some basics, but otherwise allows great latitude.

Experienced as vagueness rather than freedom, that latitude may not be appreciated. Some never understand what Harry wants from them, and some figure it out later. On the water, they will not get much of an explanation—the following exchange occurred in 2000:

Geoff Castellano '00: "Harry, it doesn't really feel any different to me."

Harry: "I don't care if you feel it, just do it!"

Michael Blomquist '03 found that if he wanted to make "real progress," rather than the small adjustments Harry asked for in daily practices, he had to go to Harry, talk about it, and get a real explanation. (Blomquist may be one of the few willing to take this step.) As an athlete John Page '02 was left puzzled by much of what Harry said to him, but the year after he graduated, when he guided an Eton College crew to a British national championship, "it was vintage Harry Parker coaching."

Harry's correctives always begin with the name of the athlete he is addressing, the first name drawn out in exaggeration: "Saaaaam Brooks ... Waaaaayne Pommen." If Harry sees no change, the name booms twice from the megaphone. "In very rare and exceptional instances, the dreaded 'Triple Name Call' was heard, where one's name would be uttered three times in succession, in increasingly exasperated tones. 'Huuugo . . . Hugo . . . HUGO!' 'Woooody . . . Woody . . .WOODY! You're not LISTEN-ING.'"

Harry is almost universally described as "patient" in his attempts to hone technique, with most lapses coming as playful mockery of the unfortunate rower. But everyone has his memory of the "one time" (or maybe two times) that Harry lost his temper and berated an individual. Harry's frustration was with those who weren't trying, and they remember his disappointment.

Matt Moeser, class of 1996: "He never quit on me and I hope he never thought I quit on him."

Wayne Pommen CP '02

Harry would sometimes use humor to draw attention to people who weren't quite toeing the line in terms of behavior. A classic example was a member of the Class of '01, who, prior to practices when the squad was meant to be stretching and warming up in the Varsity Lounge, would park himself in an armchair and wait for the practice to start. On a number of occasions, Harry remarked with a smile, "Luka! Stretching vigorously once again, I see." Squad laughter ensued. Harry's remark was said in jest but on some level it was also meant to draw attention to the fact that Luka wasn't doing what he expected and what the rest of the squad was doing.

Occasionally Harry would crack jokes, which were rare enough that they would result in uproarious laughter among those present and then within minutes would have been repeated throughout the boathouse for anyone who had missed the event. Particularly good ones would be told again for weeks, if not months and years, always in an impression of Harry's voice that most people on the squad developed. Just one example is when Greg Chiarella '02 spilled his container of Gold Bond powder on the floor in the locker room, creating a pile of white cocaine-like powder. Just then, Harry walked past, glanced at the pile, and then walked out of the room. He then poked his head back in and said with a wry smile, "Greg, I thought I told you to lay off that stuff!" It wasn't an amazing joke by most standards, but the fact that it was Harry who said it made it hilarious. There was the fact that he was cracking a joke at all, compounded by the reference to a squad member doing cocaine and him also being aware of it—a situation that bordered on the unimaginable.

Harry always avoided tearing people down unnecessarily and could see when that would be counterproductive. One great example came in 2000, when the varsity crew was doing its final race pieces before the Eastern Sprints on the weekend. In the last piece, things were going really well when the six-man caught a huge over-the-head crab, stopping the boat dead in its tracks and ruining the piece. Not exactly the confidence-builder one is looking for in the last piece before the main championships of the season. Tension ran high. I saw Harry, who was following directly behind in the launch, slam his hand down hard on the dashboard in anger and frustration, no doubt accompanied by some choice words we couldn't hear. He then picked up his megaphone, cool as a cucumber, and said in a level voice, "Mike Skey [the four-man], watch you don't throw up too much water at the finish." This always stuck in my mind. It was an incredible example of being collected in the moment and instantly matching one's response to the particular demands of the situation. Harry knew he needed to say something—otherwise we would have assumed that he was furious. He also knew that coming down on the six-man would have not only been unnecessary—the guy knew he'd screwed up—but also destructive, in that it would damage his confidence before the race. Instead, Harry made a relatively small comment to a man sitting behind him, allowing the crew to rationalize the incident and just move on. It was genius.

"Pairs and singles extravaganza!" says the day's e-mail. Sure enough, both Harry's and Charley's squads are out in small boats. The calm, sunny weather is good for it, and both coaches use pairs racing to help set the crews for the Tail of the Charles, the fall season closer two weeks from now. They will swap partners a few times, and race in the different combinations over several days. A sort of pecking order emerges—who tends to make boats go faster. Some rowers seem to go fast regardless of who they row with. Some always go slow. It is not just a reflection of size or power or fitness, or even of obvious technical ability or grace. All these are important, and a great deal of the training aims to improve them. But there are rowers who win races despite a lack of size, or a lack of strength, or a lack of "perfect form." Such a rower may be described as a "good racer," somehow able to apply himself in competitive situations more fully than others. There is a tenacity to good racers, a persistence, that Harry seems to train. Among his most common refrains are "be persistent" and "be stubborn"—don't *allow* yourself to slow down, don't *allow* your opponent to be faster.

The unexpectedly fast rower may instead have good "boat feel," a talent for using the right muscles in the right ways in the right sequence to propel a boat through the water. Despite any orthodoxy about rowing technique, despite decades of evidence about the technique of good rowers and bad, despite training machines that approximate on-the-water rowing, where athletes spend months of intense workouts with measured progress, there are still smaller, weaker rowers who can beat bigger, stronger ones. It happens all the time.

Harry lets his oarsmen pick their own pair partners. They have already done two erg tests, so they know who is similar in strength, they have a general sense of where everyone stands, and they self-select accordingly. Assistant coach Wayne Berger calls it "Darwinian." For a couple of rounds of racing, the pairs may not change at all, and then either they switch themselves, or Harry and Wayne will reassign the lineups.

The format is head-style, the distance very nearly 2,000 meters, from just above the BU Bridge up to the Weeks footbridge. The course requires the crews to steer around one long bend, then line up with the arches of the two bridges on the Powerhouse Stretch. Steering is accomplished with wires attached to a swiveled shoe controlled by one of the rowers, and it takes some time to learn well. In fact, simply rowing a pair at all takes time to learn: The smaller boat is much less stable than an eight. Any unbalanced motion from one rower's body, any stray action of blade against water, causes the boat to jolt or tip. It is a sensitive operation, and for that reason coaches value its effect on the development of boat feel. For two weeks Harry's rowers use their extra morning workouts to practice in the pairs, and occasionally row them for the normal afternoon practice. By the time they start racing, Wayne says he is pleased with the overall quality of the pairs and attributes this in part to the number of former scullers in the squad—they already know how to handle their big bodies in small boats.

For more than a week, pairs racing constitutes most of the hard work the squad does. They start on a Friday, and continue racing on Sunday and Monday. Some inclement wind comes to town in the middle of the week, so Harry has them do another 5k erg test on Tuesday and then take a couple of easy days. Racing resumes over the weekend, concluding with two sessions on Monday, with shifted lineups in between.

On the Tuesday before the Tail, Harry sends out his fours lineups. The boatings are based both on the results of pairs racing and on erg scores. Harry has a chart on his clipboard with names, times, adjustments, annotations, and multiple rankings. He does not explain his process in detail, but evidently it is not simple.

Back on the early "extravaganza" day, the crews do a simple steady-state row to get themselves used to each other. Harry follows, helping them sync their motions, but largely leaves them alone today. In the launch he is more talkative than usual, musing about college graduates, his own oarsmen included, who seek jobs with the express goal of earning huge amounts of money; Harry doesn't understand this draw to money. "What do you do with it?" he wonders. "You can only eat three meals a day, you still have to sleep some of the time. As long as you have a roof over your head . . ." He concedes, though, "I guess you could get a bigger house." Some people, he notes, seem to figure out, after making a lot, that it doesn't really do them any good, that it's really unnecessary. (A few years later, Harry tapped the generosity of his rowing alumni to fund the new Community Rowing boathouse at the top end of the Charles stretch; it was named in his honor.)

On the way home, as the crew ahead rounds a left-hand turn toward the Eliot Bridge, Harry spots a group of Canada geese on the water on the inside of the turn, on the crew's port side. He steers toward them slowly and then suddenly guns the engine, aiming to corral one goose in between the two advancing pontoons on the front of the launch. The goose flutters out of the way in time. With a gleeful smile, Harry tells me that he "got one" last week, for the first time in a long while. He knows it hit the front platform and then the engine, but doesn't know if it survived. Geese taking up space on his river are only one of Harry's peeves. Other wildlife encroach on the stronghold of Newell Boathouse itself. This year a homemade chart hangs in the shop on its own clipboard, with small black silhouettes of several animals. Tally marks, which look like Harry's work, appear next to each animal through the year: one raccoon, one goose, five squirrels, twenty-seven mice, ten rats.

Meanwhile, the freshmen have been truly united into a full squad since the Head, no longer separated by the criterion of past rowing experience. In many years Harry has had the experienced freshmen join the varsity for practice until just before the Head, while Bill spends his time with the novices. Bill must teach the technical basics, of course, but also convey a sense of the kind of strength and aerobic effort required to succeed in rowing, and look for the right attitude in these young athletes: value of the team, eagerness to work hard, ability to push current limits, positive outlook. The spring racing season is a long way off, and though normally no one is asked to leave, Bill will apportion his time and energy toward those who hold promise and who put their own energy into tapping it.

Bill Manning probably works too hard. It is difficult to arrive at Newell Boathouse at a time when Bill's Subaru wagon is not in the parking lot. He reputedly has no decoration or furnishing or food in his apartment. He does his laundry at the boathouse. He interrupts himself in mid-workout (he exercises daily, compulsively, and hard) to return to his desk and write an e-mail or make a phone call to a recruit, wearing nothing but bike shorts. His recruiting ability is arguably the reason Harvard became dominant again after 2000.

Bill worked as a college counselor and coach at a private high school in Cambridge before his intern year under Harry. Adam Holland, recently graduated, was the freshman coach that year. When Holland was set to leave, Joe Shea remembers Bill wanting the freshman job desperately, but being unsure whether to apply. During that intern year, Bill also worked as a college admissions officer. Those years of experience—working with kids applying to college, and working with college admissions on the other end—gave him crucial experience for his role as recruiter. He knows how the system works, and he knows what everyone is looking for. When he speaks with rowing prospects, he tells them the truth. He can't offer a free ride or a guaranteed admission to Harvard, so he doesn't offer them. He can tell the admissions office who he would really like, and they will consider it, but they won't necessarily do him any favors. Bill scrutinizes the prospects for the same qualities he tries to develop in his current team, the physical and mental attributes that suggest a successful Harvard student and, perhaps most importantly, a potential varsity oarsman. If he thinks he will be able to promote an applicant with admissions, he will tell him; if he can't, he will tell him that instead.

His job as coach—besides winning the Eastern Sprints, which he does with unreasonable regularity—is to develop his young rowers into men who can work with Harry. Bill sees a range of athletic maturity across the freshman squad. Some warm up before they row, some do not. Bill worries about injuries, especially during training camps or other periods of unusually hard work, and he tries to solve this by imposing a five-minute warmup on the erg. The written instructions conclude, "Don't break a sweat!" Bill's gently patronizing, admonishing style gives them the instruction that many of them need, along with a sense that really, they should be taking care of themselves. Along with athletic maturity, Bill tries to develop common sense. Harry may point out that it is cold outside, but Bill will mandate warm shirts or hats.

—◦—

The Tail of the Charles is always held the same Sunday as The Game, the football match against Yale, which is being played down in New Haven this year. Many of the rowers wish to attend, and the Tail is held early in the morning since the timing is so tight. The squads at Newell and Weld, the women's boathouse, have organized buses to take them to Yale right after the race.

On Thursday, Harry's all-squad e-mail on race strategy sets the following goals for each crew: avoid being passed, try to pass the crew in front, and place first in its "class" (each school enters several boats, ranked as A, B, C, etc.). He tells them to focus on their own rowing for the first several minutes. If the following crew appears to be moving, "respond to pressure from behind you with determination and stubbornness. Just keep pushing those puddles back and the opposing crew with them." Individual crews and coxswains may develop a more detailed race plan, with moves at particular landmarks or bridges, but it doesn't come from Harry.

A year ago Harvard's top boat won the Tail, so this year's "A" boat races with bow #1. They row a strong race, but are chased hard by Brown's top four, who is finally able to pass them in the last stage, between Weeks and Anderson Bridges. The turn at Weeks is a crucial one, and the Harvard guys think Brown steered a better course, but they nonetheless have a feeling that Brown may be, fundamentally, just a bit quicker. Brown A wins, with Boston University second, and Brown B third, less than two seconds off the winners. Harvard's top three boats finish fourth, sixth, and seventh, with Northeastern A in fifth.

Averaging the times for the top four crews, containing the rowers likely to contend for the top two eights next spring, Brown is 2.4 seconds faster than Harvard, and it is another seven seconds back to Northeastern. But just considering the top two boats, Brown is nearly four seconds ahead, Northeastern less than six behind, and BU another second behind them.

(The freshmen eights, meanwhile, have gone in for a rout: every Harvard freshman eight, heavyweight and lightweight, wins its boat class. The winning heavyweight crew is seventeen seconds faster than Brown, and the lightweights are nearly a minute ahead of Dartmouth.)

Harry tells the squad afterward that it looks like they are "roughly on par with all the strongest programs in the East," and then encourages them to outwork the competition over the winter and outrace them in the spring. In an apparent first, he schedules a meeting with each rower to talk about "training goals." They are sent home for Thanksgiving with an exhortation to do "lots of squats" if they don't have access to an erg.

When they get back, the old 5k scores are posted on the bulletin board, arranged in order of time—one list for ports, one for starboards.

They will do two more 5ks in the coming months, and Harry's goal for the team is a four- to five-second improvement over the winter. On Tuesday afternoon, after four five-minute pieces in the brisk wind, they do two 750-meter pieces on the erg. These scores are also posted the next day, and as with the 5k, Harry hopes these numbers will go down before the spring. The two distances correspond to the two kinds of muscular energy production, aerobic and anaerobic, both necessary for a rowing race. By training for a good longer performance and a good shorter performance, the body can deal with an all-out effort at an intermediate distance, the race length of 2,000 meters.

As dictated by league restrictions, the last day of November is also the day of the last fall row. To mark the occasion, it is a special practice: a class challenge race, everyone together at 3:20 p.m. They make their way down into the basin and line up for an upstream piece. There is little coaching, but a good deal of mirth. There is no selection pressure, since only class pride and bragging rights ride on the result, but it is a race, after all. The big sophomore who missed out on rowing with his class at the Head of the Charles is back in for today's row. The junior boat wins, followed by the seniors, sophomores, and freshmen.

Next week is December, and the beginning of winter training. For two months the rowers will rarely even walk out the bay doors onto the dock, and will only briefly pass through the varsity boat bay on the way to the tanks. They will not put a boat in the water again until late January, in Florida. They will not row on the Charles until February.

Steve Brooks '70 and Sam Brooks '01, Father and Son

Steve

A man of few words to be sure. And in my era (1968–1970) he was considerably less easygoing and laid-back than later—even more taciturn back then. But his presence was just overwhelming, probably helped by the distance he maintained between himself and his rowers. It was very effective. There was a sense that all you had to do was exactly what he demanded and success was inevitable. We talked among ourselves about boatings, who was up, who was down, and why things were as they were—but, with very rare exceptions, never with Harry. The only way to finally know what he was thinking was the daily boatings posted on the window at Leavitt & Peirce.

Recently, toward the end, Harry would jokingly say that when any of his rowers were paying him a tribute in public it was always more about them than him. And in that vein, I have two personal Harry stories to tell.

The first was in Mexico City during the 1968 Olympics. After a disastrous first heat, I replaced our stroke, Art Evans, who had been having problems with the altitude and had more or less passed out during the race. I had stroked the boat occasionally prior to the Games, but it was the first time that combination had actually raced. We were pretty far back through the body of the repechage but ended up sprinting through most of the field and finishing just a few inches behind the leader, earning a place in the A-final. Later that day, back in the village I was in a room discussing who-knows-what with Harry and the team manager. At some point Harry got up to leave and as he did, he turned to me and said "You stroked a good race today." Of course, we didn't do well in the final, but that's another story. In any event, it's a measure of the man's influence on me that I remember those few words like it was yesterday.

The second was in the spring of our senior year. The varsity had been picked and I was in the six-seat. We had won one race but the boat was just not feeling right. I went to Harry (I believe the only time I ever discussed boatings with him) and told him that I was unhappy with the feel of the boat and thought that I should stroke

THE SPHINX OF THE CHARLES

it. I don't remember what he said in response but certainly nothing like "How dare you?" In fact, I believe that the next day I was stroking the boat and did so for the remainder of the season. Maybe he was going to switch the lineup anyway, but I prefer to think that he had been waiting for me to step up and was pleased when I finally learned the lesson.

Harry was a major force in my life for fifty years—first thinking about going to Harvard to row for him, then actually rowing for him for my years on the varsity, and then a long and enjoyable relationship through until his death. I cannot walk into Newell without thinking of him and the role he played in my life.

I take considerable pride in the fact that Sam and I are the only father-son pair to have both rowed on Harry's varsity—thirty years apart.

Sam

One major lasting personal impact Harry had on me was when he said, at the dinner after the Yale race at Red Top in my senior year, that for the last two years the varsity had performed to its highest ability and much of that was attributable to my performance in the stroke seat. Coming from a man who generally didn't single out praise, and also considering that while we were solidly decent varsity boats we were by no means his historical top, not having won the Eastern Sprints, it meant a lot to me.

Having read Dad's note, the first half I could literally say the same (other than Harry being a young coach): the constant debates and over-analyzing among the athletes over why he picked certain boatings, and absolutely no guidance or hints from him directly—and of course the fond but anxious memories of hustling to Leavitt & Peirce after lunch to see one's fate for the day and hoping for a sign of what it meant for ultimate boatings.

I had similar one-on-one conversations with Harry regarding lineups that at first took me by surprise, assuming that Harry had no interest in what we the athletes thought. He pulled me aside one afternoon after doing pieces with a few variations of lineups and asked me point blank which felt better in the boat. I gave him my view which likely wasn't the obvious choice and yet the next day, the switch was made.

In hindsight I feel lucky to have grown up around Newell Boathouse as the son of a Harry athlete. I distinctly remember him at the Head of the Charles one year when I was a freshman in high school (and hadn't even thought about rowing yet), taking the time to chat with me, asking me how swimming was going for me. Harry himself gave me a one-on-one tour of the entire Harvard campus on my recruiting visit in high school. Fast forward to him making the effort to attend my wedding in Ireland! I didn't get fifty years with Harry but I did get literally my whole life up until his death.

Tour de Stade

SEVERAL YEARS AGO, WHILE HARRY WAS PLAYING GOLF, HIS BALL landed next to a sleeping alligator. Golfing in Florida is a nice side benefit to rowing in Florida, both recent additions to Harry's life. For many years Harvard travelled to San Diego for the "Crew Classic" regatta in late March to kick off the racing season, but it was an expensive trip. In the early 2000s the Crew Classic was abandoned in favor of a training trip to Florida, during the January vacation in between academic terms. The entire Harvard-Radcliffe rowing program—men, women, lightweights, heavyweights—started to appear at the same hotel in Cocoa Beach and train for a week in the warmth and open water that are only a dream back in Boston.

As in everything else, Harry is competitive in golf. There is a small patch of plastic grass on the floor of the workshop at Newell Boathouse, where Harry and boatman Joe Shea practice their golf swings. Sometimes in the middle of practice, while his rowers are toiling in the tanks or on the erg, you can find Harry in the shop, swinging away. Sometimes he tries to hit across the river to land on the parkland next to Memorial Drive. (One of these shots may have bounced into a car.) The golf swing is a single motion to be perfected, like the rowing stroke, and in fact this analogy has been used to convey the difficulty of rowing: imagine standing in a line with eight other golfers, and you must each hit your ball at exactly the same instant . . . and now do it thirty-five times every minute. Harry often golfs with his former rowers, and he does not like to lose.

Not long ago, while playing on the same course as some recent alumni who were a few holes ahead of him, he kept calling their cell phones to compare scores.

On that day in Florida with the alligator, Harry was playing with Joe and a member of the JV crew, Justin Webb '04. Webb points out that "every other sane person" would abandon a ball two feet away from an eight-foot alligator. But Harry walked over, remarked that "this is going to test my powers of concentration," and took his shot. It didn't go well, though, and Harry, in frustration, *hit the alligator* in the tail with his club. Says Webb: "fear a man who will attack an alligator for distracting his fairway swing!"

A week of training in Florida in January is probably a bigger benefit to the squad than a few days of travel and race preparation in March. At Newell during the winter, while much can be done on the ergs and in the tanks for individual fitness, the actual boat on the water is missing. Also missing are *crews* that can compete against each other. It seems that what Harry likes best of all is to see two crews battling it out, learning what it takes to win. So, starved of that for the two months of winter training at home, that's what the Florida trip is about.

John Page '02: "My favorite aspect about Harry was how much he loved watching competitive rowing. It really fired him up. I often wonder what keeps someone in a sport for so long. For Harry, I am convinced it was the joy of watching people pushing themselves to the limit to see who was best."

At the Harvard Business School, students study the facts of a real business case, then spend their class time debating how the business should proceed. According to Dave Fellows '74, the bad professors pit themselves against the class, but "the good professors get half of the class debating with the other half." Similarly, "Harry would get half of the crew competing with the other half—setting records for hard work, for dedication, and the like. He did not get us debating with him."

Thirty years later, here again is Justin Webb '04: "He created competition amongst the rowers ... but more than that he created competition with yourself. It wasn't about 'making the team.' It was about making yourself."

Every once in a while, perhaps more often in the early years, Harry's rowers may have felt like the Florida alligator, getting in the way of his swing. In 1975 the varsity lost the Adams Cup race to Navy, and Harry called a meeting in the tank room. When he addressed the crew, "his eyes were burning. He said, 'only three times in my career have I had a crew that was out-raced by an inferior one.'"

For Harry's more recent crews, this would be an unthinkable confrontation. The 2002 varsity were favored to win the Eastern Sprints for the first time since 1990, and when Wisconsin beat them by half a length, the Crimson accepted their silver medals on the dock in tears. Wayne Pommen '02, the team captain, recalls the following scene: "After the dust had settled and the trailer had been loaded, I found myself standing next to Harry in the parking lot as dusk fell. I felt as if we had let him down, as we had a chance to put Harvard back on top after several years and had failed to seize it. 'Sorry about that,' I said to him. He looked genuinely shocked that I would say that to him. 'No!' he said, 'It's me that feels badly for you.'"

Though he certainly assumes everyone will try their hardest at all times—he bawled out that same 2002 varsity one day, when they didn't bother to beat the JV as soundly as they could have—Harvard rowers have found that one of the strongest themes of Harry's coaching is that it is not about Harry. Though he is intensely competitive in all areas, obsessed with winning, it is the men in the boat who win and they feel this ownership. From the earliest days, he has never taken credit for the team's strengths and successes, does not see them as a benefit to himself. The team must do what he says—that is clear! But come race day, they are the ones racing. According to Fellows, "if we lost, we let each other and ourselves down"—no mention of Harry. On the other hand, crews may find themselves wanting to win "for Harry," out of their own desire to please him.

Harry does not impose much on his squad. He does not decide what music they should listen to in the erg room, though he has his personal preferences (not house or hip hop). He does not tell them what to eat, though he will weigh in on nutrition discussions: "potato skins, dark chocolate, apples (loooooooots of apples)," according to one. He does not tell them not to drink, though he would prefer that they not go overboard. He does not tell them what to wear or how to cut their hair, though he may raise an eyebrow or give an amused shake of the head at the especially flamboyant. In 1974, the "Rude and Smooth" crew spent their year-end banquet belching, mooning, cursing, running naked and drunk, all observed by a reporter. Harry sat unperturbed, "his angular face calm amid lunacy."

On the Florida trip several years ago, a junior in the third boat went on a night-time gambling cruise, three miles off shore where it is legal. Six rowers went on the boat, not telling anyone else, and enjoyed the gambling, the free drinks, and the free boat ride. At seven the next morning, when the squad gathered for practice, Harry walked up to them and asked, "So how much money did you lose last night?" "It's amazing," commented the rower. "He knows everything."

Another alumnus comments, "he knew more than we thought he knew." On the other hand, he may not know as much as he thinks he knows. After hearing of a party attended by some rowers, Harry spoke to the team captain to convey his shock that "they were doing SHOTS of VODKA!" His concern was for their health and safety, and of course any detriment to boat speed. The next day Harry, after some reflection, acknowledged to the whole squad that probably he was no more in touch with the college social scene than he had been in the 1960s, but that nonetheless heavy drinking was a bad idea if you want to go fast, and team drinking leads to discipline problems.

Harry's laissez-faire style contrasts with his own coach and mentor Joe Burk, who has been on Harry's mind this year. Burk was hospitalized on New Year's Eve with a broken leg, but even in September, on the first day of team practice, Harry talked of Joe Burk. In the same way that Harry becomes one of the strongest guiding figures in his young men's lives, Burk was that figure for Harry, his coach for four years in college and two more years in his sculling career, and then a chief rival in the collegiate coaching scene for many years thereafter.

One afternoon on the Charles the team captain, stroking a four, is complaining that the boat is leaning down too far to the port side, where his own blade is getting caught and squeezed as he extracts it from the water. He thinks it is the fault of someone else not holding his blade buried for the whole stroke. But he, the stroke seat, who is having the most trouble with the set of the boat, is not helping his own problem. When he feathers his blade, his right elbow and forearm drop down below the handle, rather than staying poised above it and pushing it down at the finish. The handle stays up high, so the blade stays low down near the water as it starts to swing backwards, and its leading edge hits the churning lip of wash left by the two-man's blade. It makes little thwacking noises on every stroke and this is clearly frustrating him. At one point his blade gets caught so badly that he entirely loses his grip on the handle, and the crew has to stop rowing for him to recover the oar. Harry speeds over to them. "That was *your fault*!!" he yells at the captain, and repeats his instructions for fixing the problem. A minute later, waiting on the other side of the river for the crew to get ready, Harry says quietly, "Joe Burk would never do that. He wouldn't express anger."

Burk was a true ascetic and expected the same from his rowers. He was morally strict, but not from a religious standpoint. He simply allowed "no indulgences, absolutely no indulgences" from himself or his athletes, recalls Harry. He drank no alcohol or caffeine. His lunch would be Jell-O and an apple from the Horn and Hardart Automat, perhaps with an ice milk. His normal weight was 196 pounds, and if he ever reached 200, he stopped eating. With the rowing squad, the rules were clear even if not always stated explicitly. If you deviated from Burk's expectations you would feel his "full moral authority" on you. "Why would you do that?" Burk would say. "What made you do that?"

Joe Burk's parents were farmers from New Jersey. Travelling to England to watch their son race his single at the Henley Royal Regatta, they stayed at the Red Lion Inn, in the thick of the regatta week's bustle. They hated it. Burk, likewise, though obviously drawn to the prestige and the competition at Henley, was averse to the pomp and gilding of the event. Coaching the University of Pennsylvania at Henley, he warned his rowers away from the social trappings, preferring that they show up for practice and then return to their quarters in Twyford, two train stops away.

Harry Parker was happy to do so. After the stifling heat of a Philadelphia summer, England's cool weather in late June of 1955 made him want to curl up in bed, which is what he did in between rows. He was not naturally drawn to the carousing behavior of his Penn teammates, who rented bicycles and proceeded to get lost trying to reach Oxford. Alcohol, of course, was forbidden to them. At a reception in Hamburg, during a post-Henley tour in Germany, Coca-Cola was served, and even this was considered off-limits. "No indulgences."

Harry has been known to indulge. He enjoys a beer, drinks champagne after Harvard-Yale wins, eats the occasional doughnut. Many who knew them in the 1950s found that Harry was like a reflection of Joe Burk, with similar work ethic and personal style. Coach Allen Rosenberg said they were "like twins." David Halberstam concluded that Harry "felt at home with Burk because this was so natural a manner for him. He was emulating what he already was." Harry agrees that he did not imitate Burk. Many years after leaving the University of Pennsylvania, upon meeting another former Penn rower from the same era, Harry was struck by how clearly he mimicked Burk's mannerisms and speaking style. Harry doesn't feel that he did this himself.

Personal discipline came naturally to Harry, since it served the driving passion for rowing that he discovered at Penn. But Harry was not really a follower. In payment for his ROTC scholarship, Harry served on a Navy destroyer out of Newport for many months. There the discipline, the uniforms, "all that crap," were unappealing. He was always on the verge of getting in trouble. (Otherwise, he enjoyed his time in the Navy well enough: He went around the world on the destroyer and served as onshore liaison for the Marines in Beirut in 1958.)

Though he is not "outgoing and friendly" as he describes Joe Burk, Harry may consider himself approachable in the same way. He is surprised to learn that a girls crew from Brookline High School, taking shelter inside Newell during a thunderstorm, are so intimidated by him that they dare not say hello when Harry walks by. "Unbelievable!" he says, when I tell him. Most of his own oarsmen do not feel that they can talk casually with him—conversations are brief and uncomfortable. The total time talking with the captain on issues related to the squad may add up to fifteen minutes for the entire year.

Nonetheless Harry adopted Burk's style of being addressed by his first name, very unusual for the 1950s. "Coaches had to be authority figures; they had to be called 'mister' or 'coach.' Joe just didn't want anything to do with that. Occasionally you would have some who had a hard time calling him 'Joe' so they would call him 'sir' or 'mister' or occasionally 'coach' and he would turn around and say, 'yes, athlete?' Or if they called him 'Mr. Burk' he would say, 'yes, Mr. So-so-and-so.' So it was quite clear that he wanted to be called 'Joe.'" And Harry feels the same way.

The atmosphere at Newell Boathouse, for all its intensity and sometimes holy silence, is welcoming and inclusive. The former rowers and other guests who use the boathouse, though they may tread carefully, are made to feel at home. In many ways the atmosphere Harry promotes is one of family. His own wife, daughter, and dog are virtually members of the team, moving easily among the rowers.

It is the aura, more than anything else, that keeps others away. While Harry does not set out to fraternize with his athletes, they themselves shrink from risking more closeness, cowed by the minimal responses, the intensity of his attention, the sense that you must say the right thing. Justin Webb '04, to the amazement of his classmates, effortlessly ignored the barrier and had an easy, joking relationship with Harry (including the Florida golf game with the alligator), while he was rowing in the junior varsity. Similarly, a young intern coach from the Harvard women's team would tease Harry constantly. A playfulness emerged when he encountered someone willing to challenge him, to match his acuity. Most do not find themselves in a position to risk it.

Harry is like a stern and distant father with high standards—standards that the rowers want fervently to meet. The distance does not appear to be a calculation in order to be a strong leader, but simply his personality. He has always interacted with them in the ways that were natural to him: teaching and training them, perhaps racing against them on the ski trail or the steps of the stadium. He is not a counselor or a chum. As a student, Harry would walk the eight miles from Philadelphia to Bala Cynwyd to talk rowing with Joe Burk. It is hard to imagine the scene if a Harvard oarsman walked the eight miles from Cambridge to Winchester with the idea of a chat with Harry.

Joe Harvey '89 invokes an essential theme from *Walden* to characterize Harry's life and his teaching: "Simplicity. The pursuit of boat speed. The production of the very fastest crews he could assemble. The building, year on year, of a program that resembled Harry not as an individual, but that reflected the purity, the simplicity, of his vision and focus.

"Harry set the standard for us. He held himself, always, to the very highest test, modeling for us, to the very end, how we might live. Somehow relentless and yet gracious at the same time, stubborn and caring, serious and full of joy, complex and yet purely focused, proud and yet wary of the spotlight, competitive but inclusive in his vision, and deeply respectful of each individual he encountered."

Over the course of a weekday afternoon in December that extends into the dark early evening, four groups of eight rowers make their way in turn down to the "Old Tanks." They have warmed up lightly on the erg and done some squats and back extensions as directed on the bulletin board. Coxswains are scheduled, too; though obviously there is no steering to be done, they help keep time and run the practice. The rowers start off with a stroke-length progression: arms only, arms and body, full slide. The oars are wood, heavier than the usual carbon fiber, so some of the resistance is from the inertia of the oar itself. A floor is built up around the sunken "boat," a walking gallery at the height of the rowers' heads. Harry walks along the sides, looking down closely at the rowing. Now, during the warmup, he tells them what to feel for. He wants the shoulders to stay down, the elbows to draw past the body, rather than sticking out to the side. There is a mirror directly in front of the line of seats, and two sliding mirrors on the sides, allowing a couple of rowers at a time to see their bodies in motion. "Swing the body, then draw the arms . . . use the lower back before bending the arms." Harry places his right hand on his own lower back as he says this, though the rower he is talking to cannot see him.

They row for a few minutes at "paddle" pressure, have a short break, then do a ten-minute piece at three-quarter pressure. During one session this afternoon, Harry tells the coxswain that he is giving commands "too energetically," and that he needs to focus on pronouncing the words, so the oarsmen can understand him. He has the coxswains give the commands to start and stop the piece and change intensities, and tell the men how much time they have left in the piece. After the coxswain starts them off again, Harry tells him "that was better" with a nod, and walks off down the side of the tank. The coxswain is smiling but a little shaken, too.

The group does one ten-minute piece, then a couple of eight-minute pieces at higher pressure. Then upstairs to the ergs, where they do two five-minute pieces with part of the monitor's display covered with white tape. They can see the elapsed time and their stroke-rate, which is supposed to be twenty-six, but they have to base their "full pressure" intensity on their own perceived effort, not on a number on the screen. Wayne Berger (Harry's assistant with the varsity squad) and the coxswain talk them through it, and at the end of the second piece, they are spent. They bear expressions of pain, of despair.

Directly behind them are similar expressions on the faces of the freshmen, who are spending a full hour on their row of ergs: three twenty-minute pieces at prescribed five-hundred-meter split-times given to them by Bill. Do whatever you have to do to make your splits, he tells them. Sweat pools on the varnished floor below their machines. On their way out of the boathouse some time later, they warn Bill's next group against being gung-ho and trying to beat the splits. Just do the number you're supposed to, they say. It's hard enough just to do that.

A few days later, Harry's men are back in the Old Tanks: ten-minute pieces at three-quarter pressure with five minutes' rest in between. At the end of one piece Harry says, "Heart rates! . . . Go!" and while the rowers hold their fingers to their necks he counts fifteen seconds on his wristwatch. "Stop!" He looks at each man down the line, and they tell him how many beats they counted. "Good!" he says. He likes the numbers he is hearing: thirty-nine, forty, forty-one (meaning: 156, 160, 164 beats per minute). He tells them they are rowing at the right level. "You could keep doing that forever, right?"

Sometimes Harry walks around the tank, sometimes he leans against the wall near the stroke seat, sometimes he stands halfway down the line, elbows resting behind him on the rail through which the mirror slides, staring at one rower for a few minutes. Sometimes he sits in the single wooden chair in the corner and gazes at the whole group from a three-quarter angle, with legs crossed, yet ready to spring up at any time.

As a training tool, Harry likes the Old Tanks. If both sets of tanks are available, he will use the old ones. Wayne Berger says that at Brown they have two tanks, just like here at Harvard, but they don't use them—they spend the whole winter on the ergs. Charley seems more likely to use the new tanks than Harry, focused as he is on precision and efficiency of oar- and blade-work. Harry's men spend the winter doing five- to ten-minute pieces in the Old Tanks, feeling the resistance, the weight. The tank recreates the asymmetrical sweeping motion, the lifting and dropping of the oar, the need to match the slide speed of the other rowers, and the visual feedback to learn timing at the catch and finish.

The various elements of a rowing boat in the water are all turned around in the tanks. Seats slide, oars swing, water splashes. But the oarlocks are fixed to a concrete ledge, the oars have only the outlines of a blade at the end, with a big hole in the middle. There is painted wood planking *under* the water, on the floor of the trough. The water is deepest out where the blades get buried, and then the trough floor angles upwards to the edge of the concrete ledge. As the blades churn the water rhythmically, a series of waves wash on the inner shoreline, break, recede, and get subsumed by the next wave. It is a lot like waves on a beach, and in fact the whole scene, rowers included, has the mesmerizing quality of a rocky coastline. Sometimes there is a hovering fog of exhalation and perspiration. It billows through the louvered windows to the snowy, quiet dock outside.

To stoke the competitive fires, Harry creates opportunities. Over the Christmas vacation, when they will be on their own to stay in shape, there is a "holiday points contest." Careful guidelines give the point values assigned to amounts of work, be it erging, cycling, skiing, running, weightlifting. Sometimes scores are pooled between partners. The men keep their own logs, turn them in when they return in January, and wait for Harry to tally the results. It is an honor system, and there is little cheating. Some take it very seriously.

But before that, on the Saturday before the winter break starts, nearly every athlete in the boathouse competes in the Newell Triathlon. The events are 7,500 meters on the erg, a 4.7-mile run, and a full circuit of the Harvard Stadium. The run takes them along the banks of the Charles, around the bends, and over the bridges they see every day on the river. Those coxswains and coaches who are not themselves participating take times for each leg of the event, and the results are compiled afterward. Start times are staggered throughout the morning, since there are not enough ergs to go around. Winning times are around seventy-five minutes.

In a note to his freshmen rowers, Bill Manning calls the stadium Harvard's "secret weapon," and says it has helped improve generations of oarsmen. It was built during Harvard's riverside building boom a hundred years ago, which produced a trio of athletic landmarks: Newell Boathouse in 1900, the stadium in 1903, and Weld Boathouse in 1907. Quite apart from its remarkable presence, rising like an ivy-covered concrete Colosseum from the flat of Soldier's Field, and the magnificent sense of space within its grand horseshoe, the stadium is also a training tool for athletes across many disciplines. The seats are just big steps, fifteen inches high and thirty deep, so the stadium is like a U-shaped Incan terrace, divided by narrow stairways into thirty-seven sections. Each is marked with a large painted number at the top, and small letters mark the rows, from the bottom to the top. They go from A to Z and then continue from AA to PP.

When you run the Harvard Stadium you ascend the seats, touch the number at the top of the section, run down the stairways between sections, then up the next section of seats, gradually working your way around the big horseshoe. Among the rowers at least, a full running of the stadium is called a "Tour de Stade." In a curious linguistic twist, sections are referred to plurally as "stadia": The bulletin board might give instructions for the post-row workout as "15 stadia." Running a portion of the stadium, anything from several stadia to a full tour, is a common post-row workout, or an additional workout to do in the morning. Ollie Rando '95 says the stadium got him in shape when he was learning to row: technique on the water, a stadium tour off the water. At the Head of the Charles in October, a group of lightweight alums reminisced about the triathlon, the stadium, and Jesse Elzinga '01, a tremendously fit athlete who broke the Triathlon record his senior year. The record was previously held by Andy Sudduth '85, often called the greatest Harvard oarsman. They think Elzinga ran the stadium in under fifteen minutes. A full tour for a heavyweight is usually around twenty minutes, and it is hard, panting, burning work. After a few sections are complete, you find that the trip down the stairs no longer lets you recover from the trip up. This intense aerobic endurance and the explosive use of the legs and core are ideal for training a rower.

The weather doesn't look promising for running the Triathlon on the usual Saturday—there has been freezing rain, and it will get colder again on the weekend. Harry's oarsmen are given the option of doing the Triathlon events on Wednesday, or some altered version on Saturday: three 7,500-meter erg pieces with rest in between, or two 7,500s and the run, but no stadium. Most pick the last option.

Harry himself only spends time on the erg in the weeks leading to the Triathlon. Though this year he is recovering from a hernia operation, in most years he still competes, and he does not finish last. There is often a bet between Harry and his squad—he will beat their average time, or a weighted average, or some other mathematical concoction. The price of losing is a bodily sacrifice to the river gods, in the December cold. Usually he wins this bet.

(By contrast, stories from Harry's days at the University of Pennsylvania have him quickly following Joe Burk for a dive into the freezing Schuylkill River in the winter. Whether this was to demonstrate the safety of rowing in the cold, or to prove manhood, varies in the recollection.)

Three days of winter training:

Thursday: 10k at "Triathlon pace" on the erg, followed by 20 stadia.

Friday: 10 times: 1 minute at three-quarter pressure, 1 minute full pressure, 1 minute rest, in the Old Tanks, followed by 12 stadia.

Saturday: 4 times 10 minutes in the old tank: (1) two-thirds pressure building to full, (2) all at three-quarters, (3) three-quarters building to full, (4) all at full. Then, 10 minutes at rate 24 on the erg.

In the early 1960s you would not have found such a busy Newell Boathouse on a December afternoon. Or rather, the *oarsmen* would not be so busy. They would sign up for a daily session in the tanks (there was just the one set, latterly designated Old). The session would last for twelve minutes, and then they would go back to the rest of their lives. It may have been a hard twelve minutes, since all rowing was full pressure in those days, but only twelve minutes nonetheless. In his early days at Harvard, Harry would supervise these sessions, and it was so boring ("stultifying") that he would fall asleep.

Harry's first year of coaching was a losing one. The 1961 Harvard freshmen had a 1-3 dual racing season in the spring, and finished sixth at the Eastern Sprints. The printed program for the Harvard-Yale Regatta that year lists the personnel for each university, reporting succinctly, "Harry L. Parker, Freshman Coach," and offering no further information. From that year on, Harry always came out ahead. Next year the freshmen improved to 3-1, and this time finished second at the Sprints to Cornell. In 1963, the Harvard-Yale program reads, "Harry L. Parker, Acting Head Coach." For with the sudden death of varsity coach Harvey Love, Harry had been asked to take over for the spring. Coxswain Ted Washburn '64 describes that spring as "mayhem." It was very clear, he says, that Harry was "figuring things out as he went along. It must have been horrendous for him." Their spring record was 3-2, and they did not reach the Grand Final at Sprints, won by Cornell. (Meanwhile Lawrence Coolidge, the lightweight coach, had taken over Harry's freshmen, and they were "untouchable" in winning the Sprints that year. Washburn suspects that would not have happened if Harry had stayed with them.)

The varsity floundered through the spring of 1963, trying different racing stroke rates, figuring out what kind of rowing felt good to them. After the Sprints, this stopped. Nothing had worked, so they started with the basics, rowed sixteen miles every day, and "built a long, muscular, well-honed, well-executed stroke at low cadences." By the time the

Harvard-Yale race came in June, the varsity eight were "an honest-to-God four-mile crew," says Washburn. The *Boston Globe* decided that Harvard had been "too big for that distance of 2000 meters," and the *Herald* announced that they were "geared to upset" Yale. Harry told the *Herald* that he was "hopeful," and there had been "no bad omens." They had the endurance, the power, and the confidence to outlast and mow down Yale who, a few weeks before, had bested them. "And that," says Washburn, "was the beginning of it all."

The 1964 varsity went undefeated in their collegiate races, and then they did it again in 1965. Joe Burk called his protégé's varsity eight "the greatest American crew there has ever been, college or club." By then Burk was considered the "dean of current college coaches," a title he held for another decade and which Harry then took over, with hardly any intervening holders. The Princeton coach said he had "never seen a crew move a boat so fast." The MIT coach said he was "shell-shocked." Harry was "the only coach in the East this year not to heap praise on his oarsmen." He did concede, "They are undoubtedly faster than any previous *college* crew," and elsewhere that "it's a little hard to believe they can be this good."

The *Globe* ran a four-day series called "Harvard's 'Wonder Crew.'" It described Harry's personality, coaching style, and relationship with the rowers: "a soft-voiced, modest, non-blustery type" who treats his charges "like colleagues engaged in a joint venture." It described, with diagrams, the equipment and rigging changes that Harry had put into place: the shorter Stampfli boat, the newer, stubbier "shovel" blades that were easier to handle, "making for niftier oarsmanship," and the "bucket" rigging arrangement, placing the four- and five-seats on the same side of the boat, instead of a strict alternation of ports and starboards down the length of the shell. It reviewed their rowing style in some detail: constant slide speed, no "exasperated lay back," not high-stroking, not low. It profiled the personality of the crew, who "let their hair grow. And a couple of them find it convenient to wear head-bands to keep the stuff out of their eyes." Of Harry Parker, the article concluded that "since the spirit and the soul is as important in rowing as rigging, he's the man for the job." And though taking over the head coaching position from Harvey Love was initially considered temporary, "the square-jawed, understating Parker should be good more or less forever." It is hard to find a more prescient statement than that.

What had Harry done? Just about everything. He tried new things. He tried the Aylings oars in 1964, the Stampfli boat in 1965. When another local coach visited Germany and brought back some oars, Harry tried them (he liked how with these oars, as in the Old Tanks, you could feel the weight of the shaft and hear a satisfying noise—"chook!"—at the catch). "This sport tends to be conservative," Harry told *Time* magazine. "I'm inclined to try things out to see what works best." This is still true in his fifth decade of coaching. Kathy Delaney Smith, the women's basketball coach at Harvard, worked with Harry on an athletic policy committee for the university. She sees Harry as set in his ways, and yet not close-minded. One of his "ways" is to seek improvement. "He is so brilliant that if he decides something has value he can accomplish it in about seven seconds."

Harry watched other crews. An impression of a crew racing, or an oarsman at a certain phase of the rowing stroke, would become a paradigm for how to mold his own men. Coaching a coxed four of Harvard men at the Tokyo Olympics in 1964, he watched the German crews and, even more so, the Russian four. Back in Cambridge, he changed the Harvard rhythm. It was mostly the recovery, which he smoothed out, eliminating the rush out of the finish and the pause before the catch. The 1965 cover story from *Sports Illustrated* described how they "combine their stroke, their recovery and their catch in a single, short, virtually uninterrupted motion." Others noted the "solidness of the Crimson catch," the "precision of its bladework," and the "immaculate release." The Princeton coach was so impressed by Harvard's new style that he immediately imposed it on his own crew, on the Monday after Harvard "thrashed" them in the Compton Cup.

Harry changed the training. He wrote in the *Boston Herald* in 1964 that college rowing was "at a crossroads." It had typically been college crews who represented the United States at the Olympics, but in 1964 the undefeated Harvard, who had been openly focusing on the Olympic Trials, lost to Vesper Boat Club. It was a bitter defeat, and it began a long rivalry between Harry and the Vesper coach, Allen Rosenberg. American dominance in international rowing had ended in the 1950s with the rise of the Russians and the Germans, largely influenced by Karl Adam's "rather startling innovations" at the Ratzeburg Ruderclub, some of which had been adopted by Vesper. Harry described how Harvard, too, to be effective in the world arena, had started "following the example of the Europeans." They trained "hard and consistently throughout the year." They rowed in pairs and singles, went on group runs, and used the new weight-training equipment upstairs at Newell, all "in an organized program." They ran the Harvard Stadium, sometimes with bags of sand hung from their shoulders. The basic conditioning method on the water (and in the tanks) was interval training, alternating stretches of faster and slower rowing without periods of complete rest in between. The Europeans did this, and so did Joe Burk at Penn. Within a few years, Burk would say, "Harry has taken the best of the European techniques and applied them to Harvard rowing." The days of twelve-minute tank sessions were over.

Later, Harry again followed Burk in adopting German methods, but this time it was the opposite end of the training scale: long, low-intensity rows. There had been "no sustained sub-max training at all until the 70s," says Harry. Joe Burk read about the extended steady-state sessions that the East Germans were using, and instituted them at Penn. It took Harry and other college coaches a few more years to pick up on it; today, this is the bread-and-butter of rowing workouts. Burk went to extremes that Harry did not: "Joe would do twenty miles. We never did that." Occasionally, for the adventure, Harry would take his crews through the locks below the Boston Museum of Science, under the Charlestown Bridge, and into Boston Harbor, perhaps clear across to Quincy. But this was in the early days, and they did it at full pressure, possibly too hard to get the right training effect.

The rowing community was split at this time on the subject of stroke-rates. Ratzeburg rowed high, around forty strokes per minute, and Vesper matched them in this. But Harry kept his crews lower, typically thirty-four or even lower, and was criticized for it. Tom Bolles, former Harvard crew coach and subsequently athletic director, felt that it was inefficient to row as high as forty for a two-kilometer race, and that a powerful crew at thirty-two can go faster. Others considered this opinion "outmoded," suggesting that a higher stroke-rate is preferable and merely requires, to be feasible, a shorter stroke in the water. Harry felt that it was more about manpower than technique. For all the hype about Ratzeburg, when they raced as a guest with the best American colleges in 1963 they were essentially matched by Cornell. And though Vesper beat Harvard at the Olympic Trials and again at Henley in 1965, Harvard went straight to the international regatta at Lucerne and won it, beating Russia and Yugoslavia and amazing the European crowds just as they had amazed those at home.

In those early years, Joe Burk captured Harry's approach to coaching: "He's a student . . . constantly striving to learn more and teach more." Recently Harry had indeed been Burk's own student, as they worked together in Philadelphia, sculling side by side, discussing training, technique, race strategies. "As a sculler," said Burk, "you learn to think for yourself and be resourceful." Once truly out on his own, leading Harvard, Harry worked to outpace his own teacher.

So the rowing world (and some of the rest of the world) paid attention to the innovations in technique and equipment that Harry brought to Harvard rowing. "I truly believe that Harry is ten years ahead of his time," said Al Rosenberg. "By 1975, I'll be surprised if every college coach isn't using his equipment and training routine." Another accurate prediction. And yet, as identified in England's *Rowing* magazine, Harry's very identity, the "unique influence" of his personality and character, was perhaps the biggest new asset at Newell boathouse. With Ted Washburn's help, he found athletes with "great ambition and enthusiasm," and then used his innate talent for "converting eagerness into oarsmanship."

"To me," said Harry, "rowing is only 1 to 2 percent oars. The most important thing is the oarsmen themselves, and the approach they take to the sport." Over and over, observers echoed the *New York Times*: "he gives all the credit to his men." Over and over, Harry talked of his "outstanding group" of "darn good oarsmen" and their "high degree of motivation." And they, in turn, praised him right back. "He is such an incredibly fine fellow, as well as a great coach." "He gets across easily. He understands. He's patient." Furthermore, he "hardly ever uses the word 'crew' or 'boat.'

He emphasizes our commitment to the whole squad." A photo from *Sports Illustrated* shows Harry kneeling next to a rower in the Old Tanks, explaining a technical point. Apart from the hair on his head, the scene could be from last winter. "Harry won't let us row badly."

Harry did not imitate Joe Burk's personality. Nor, when learning to scull under his tutelage, did he adopt Burk's upright style or exaggerated stroke-rates. If anything, thinks Harry, it was the coaching that he initially, consciously, patterned after his longtime mentor. Their crews faced each other every year in the Adams Cup, repeatedly fought each other for gold at the Eastern Sprints, and battled to a photo finish at the 1968 Olympic Trials ("Isn't that great!" said Burk, looking at the photo. "Isn't that beautiful!" said Harry). For the last three years of the 1960s, the last three years of Burk's coaching career, his varsity won the IRA championships—because Harvard was busy racing Yale. Joe Burk died on January 13, 2008, following surgery on a broken leg. Penn AC, his old club in Philadelphia, named a new single scull after him. The University of Pennsylvania commissioned a bronze relief sculpture at the boathouse. Harry's old teacher, mentor, and friend was gone. He didn't talk much about it, but later he wrote to Joe Harvey '89:

"He was indeed a remarkable man and a very important person in my life. And, as you suggest, he no doubt had a great influence on me as a person and as a coach, greater perhaps than I ever realized. I hope I have done him justice."

Gregg Stone '75

I was neither an ideal rowing candidate nor an ideal oarsman, but one of Harry's strengths was that he took an interest in oarsmen throughout his program. While the press and the alumni might have focused on varsity races and records, Harry was equally pleased to have an outperforming 3V as a great varsity.

In the summer of 1973 I stopped by the boathouse on my way home from a lousy performance in a sailing regatta. I confessed to Harry that I had begun to doubt that I would ever be an Olympic sailor. He pointed to an older Shea single in a very high rack and told me to take it down and to learn to row it.

The next summer he offered to drive in from Winchester a few times a week to row with me. I suspect his coaching techniques with me were the same as Joe Burk had used with him. He said almost nothing, and to the best of his ability he started every piece up by enough to stay ahead at the finish. Late in the summer Harry invited me to his house in Winchester for dinner, where he told me that the nationals were in Orchard Beach the next week, and while the entries were closed, would I go down to race if he was able to enter me in the intermediate single. I thought of the parties and sailing I would miss and my stature in front of The Man, and said yes, hoping that it wouldn't work out.

Of course, Harry did get me an entry, in the senior single. At the start of the heat I rowed my thumbs into each other for a sharp pain and no reward before I fumbled off in last place. Fortunately most of the other contestants tired and I squeaked into a qualifying second place at the finish. A bit later, off the water, a Harvard teammate came up to me and asked if I had seen Harry. I said no, he was at home. The teammate corrected me and said that Harry was at the finish of my race, jumping around and clearly excited. Then he drove home.

Hovey Kemp '76

My senior year rolled around and we faced the loss of six incredibly talented seniors who had graduated the prior year. What I remember best about that year was the way Harry managed the crew and the expectations, which must have been pretty low at the start. Harry, dubbed "The Weird One" long before we got there, really must have coached his brains out getting us together and making us fast. We were not long on technique and had a few races where crabs and other mishaps slowed us down. But all through the season Harry encouraged us to forget about the "gods" that had graduated and just work together to make the boat go fast. He was patient as hell through the fall and winter. He never gave up on us and he truly encouraged us to have fun and enjoy each other as we worked together to practice hard and race harder. End result: We surprised everyone and went undefeated and again won the "unofficial" national title.

I absolutely credit Harry as being one of the most influential men in my life. Still feel that way. There was my dad, and one or two mentors in my professional career who deserve a lot of credit in making me who I am, but those three years working my tail off for Harry and the H crew program were incredibly formative as well. Harry never got so close to us to where I felt my personality or soul was being sculpted by him . . . nor did he rule our lives in any kind of tyrannical manner. We did what was needed to be done to make the boat because he showed us the way. He showed us how to get there, how to be disciplined in our training, how to push ourselves each day to our limits, and how to be accountable to and rely on the other guys in the boat. He did not seem to focus or intrude on our lives outside the boathouse, but he clearly expected us to bring our "A" game every day to practice. He kept his distance and simply focused on rowing techniques, fitness, choosing the best boat combinations, and race preparations.

Harry was incredibly competitive and although we all had brought plenty of our own to the boathouse every day, his bright fire heated us all. Fall circuit runs, running stadiums, racing in cross-country ski races in New England in the winter, sitting in a boat on the Charles as he constantly rode me to improve some aspect of my technique, feeling his steely gaze as I did an erg piece or across the water when he didn't say anything at all, his minimalist pre-race speeches . . . everything contributed so that when I was on the starting line or in the heart of a very competitive race, I found myself calm and ready to race—knowing that I was prepared, trusting that my teammates were also, knowing that if I pushed myself to my limits the other guys in the boat would be doing the same, and confident that we would beat the other boat . . . that was the culmination of all of Harry's focus and efforts to make me believe I could do it. And all that stays with you, and having been forged in Harry's fire, tackling life's other challenges doesn't seem so hard.

Harry Parker in the two-seat, University of Pennsylvania, 1955. UNIVERSITY OF
PENNSYLVANIA

In the single, 1960. VESPER BOAT CLUB

1961 Harvard freshmen. The first crew Harry coached and his only losing season.
TED WASHBURN

Newell Boathouse: "grim and grand."

The Old Tanks.

Harry and the "Wonder Crew," 1965. SPORTS ILLUSTRATED

Harvard (near) and Pennsylvania approach the finish line of the 1968 Olympic trials, dead level.

THE
OARSMAN
Official publication of The National Association of Amateur Oarsmen   March, 1972

**1972
NATIONAL
TEAM
COACH**

Harry Parker

Coach of the first national team, 1972. THE OARSMAN/NATIONAL ASSOCIATION OF AMA-
TEUR OARSMEN

The undefeated 1974 "Rude and Smooth" varsity.

The 1985 varsity in practice at Henley: National Champions and winners of the Grand Challenge Cup. DAN GROUT

From a display of Henley results at Newell Boathouse.

Heading upstream in the Basin past the MIT boathouse.

Race day morning message.

The bulletin board in the locker room, the morning of the Compton Cup.

CHAPTER 5—FEBRUARY

Keep Digging

THE FIFTH OF FEBRUARY PROMISES A "NICE AFTERNOON!" ACCORDING TO Harry's e-mail to the squad. It's less than forty degrees out, and it was drizzling earlier in the day. The sky is gray; the water is darker gray. Occasional sheets of ice, the size and thickness of plywood, float downstream along the river banks. MIT's floating docks were pulled up at the end of November and won't go back in until the river is safely thawed. But the dock at Newell stays in all winter, and once January is over any usable water will be exploited.

As the new term starts, Harry sends out an e-mail urging the rowers to avoid taking classes that start at nine or earlier—they will interfere with morning practices. And a week later, to underline the point, he notes that classes that meet Tuesday and Thursday at ten will have final exams the morning of the day before the Eastern Sprints, interfering with travel plans and adding stress and logistical trouble to an important race weekend.

Here are some other e-mail subject lines: Very Well Done! Thursday . . . Yea, ?sun! Friday . . . Wow! Results . . . Well Done! Monday . . . A Glorious Fall Day! Tuesday . . . clearing on the way. Monday Pairs. Nice Day! Friday . . . uugh! Monday Times . . . and. NICE DAY! Friday . . . yeah Rain! Nice Morning! Monday . . . Yea warmth! 1:45! Monday . . . the thaw begins! Tuesday PM Windy! Great Day! 2:00 PM!

Harry started sending daily practice e-mails ten years ago. The body of the e-mail may have other announcements or information, but mainly it is a list of who is scheduled to practice at what times. Here is a typical one:

2:20 Ash, Otto, Rum, Laus, Ant, Cann, Hirt, Stroh, Flem

3:10 Tope, Ken, Gaw, Heff, John, JT, Mead, Bee, Web, Brug?

4:15 Kelly, Kit, Morg, Joe, Liv, Sch, Bay, Vuk, Ruet, Gilch, RX Ivan, Tooth, Mah, CF

No time given: MF OYO Atta, Drew, Andrea, JL

Three eights, listed with the coxswain first, then from stroke to bow, are rowing on this afternoon. Four are sick or injured ("RX"), and four are "On Your Own." Harry composes this during the morning, working from the information from the day before. Essentially the same list will be handwritten and posted on the bulletin board in the locker room, and when the men come to practice they will write down their earliest availability for the following day. That is the piece of paper Harry will bring back to his desk to make up the next schedule. Everyone must get used to Harry's shorthand for their names. They are easier to decipher in the typed e-mail than on the scribbled list on the bulletin board. You may only get two letters, so you had better recognize them. If you are the captain you may be designated "CP," and if you are the Master of Protocol, you may be "MP."

Before e-mail, Harry (and his predecessors back to Tom Bolles in the 1930s) would give the daily lineup to a student manager, who would walk it up JFK Street (originally "Boylston") to the Harvard Square tobacconists Leavitt & Peirce, where he would tape it to the inside of the front window. This was also how crew announcements were made. To learn if you were in the varsity or the JV, you went to the window at Leavitt & Peirce. (Anyone else walking down Mass. Ave. would also know, if they cared to look.) Blocker Meitzen saved Harry's very last L&P posting, and framed it alongside a black and white photograph of eager oarsmen crowding around the storefront.

⌐━━⌐

Often the coaches spend their days in February encouraging the river to clear up. They start with the small patch of water by the boathouse, kept unfrozen all winter by an underwater bubbler, and work their way out. There are a few methods for breaking ice, depending on the thickness. If it is very thin and brittle, a small metal launch can plow right through, crunching a path and sending little ice flecks skittering across the surface. Harry drives, with another coach standing in the bow, and as the launch cuts a path, he commands, "rock!" A vigorous left-right stomping motion creates waves that push out on both sides and cut a wider swath through the ice. It is not easy work for the rocker. Once there is a long enough stretch of free water to get the launch up to a good speed, a rolling wake parallel to the ice edge will push the ice up and down, and break off whole strips as the launch goes by. If the ice is thicker, it may require getting out and hacking at it, perforating it with a metal pike until it weakens. The small scraps of ice melt more quickly and are carried downstream by the current.

A few years ago I was among the group of coaches who had cleared a stretch of river less than a mile in length, starting below the boathouse and reaching upstream and around the corner, nearly to Eliot Bridge. A couple of Harry's crews were out, doing five-minute loops up and down this bit of water, while Harry and I worked away on the ice at the top end, running the small metal launch up against the ice edge, jumping on it, breaking off chunks and nudging them downstream. The launch motor failed and even Harry couldn't start it again, so we started working our way back to the boathouse, Harry using a canoe paddle while I pushed off ice floes with a vintage iron-tipped pike. As we emerged from the sea of floes, one of Harry's crews was nearby. A rower called out, "You look like something from *Moby Dick!*" but Harry shook his head and gruffly yelled, "It's *Shackleton!*" He had in fact just seen a film about Ernest Shackleton's epic voyage in the Antarctic. And it is an apt comparison, given the *Endurance* crew's devotion to Shackleton and his ability to respond to changing, hopeless circumstances and navigate the route to salvation. Harry seems like the sort of man who could do this. (In 2005, amid rumors about whom President Bush would appoint to direct the post-Katrina effort, writer Jesse Kornbluth compiled on the *Huffington Post* a list of "10 Americans who could head the reconstruction better than Karl Rove." Harry Parker was number seven.)

—◆—

Now, on this day in early February, the earlier afternoon practice slot has two eights rowing together, one in a yellow Empacher shell, the other a white Pocock. The Empacher pushes off the dock a few minutes later than the Pocock, and then doesn't turn with the other crew to come back downstream in tandem. Circling in the launch in front of the boathouse, frustrated with having to hold up one crew and wait around for the other, Harry scolds both coxswains for not sticking together. "When I have two crews out I expect you to stay near each other."

As they do the usual series of warmup tens and twenties, it looks like the work in Florida has been effective. Though the crews are the usual mish-mash of whoever is available at this particular time slot, there is a look of uniformity about them. Oars and bodies are moving together, blades are staying tight to the water, burying together. Harry calls out a couple of the rowers for blades that square too early, then hover in the air before coming down for the catch, probably a little late on the others, probably missing some water. He wants the blade to "bury as soon as it's square."

Once through the bridge and past the BU boathouse, Harry has the crews gather at the finish line, pointing near the middle of the bridge at Mass. Ave. When they are level, he has them sit at the catch, like they would at the start of a race, and they go off together at a firm pressure, staying level until Harry marks the real start of the piece with his characteristic "ooooooooonn this one." They race at rate twenty-six over the full 2k course in the basin, just over six minutes, during which Harry makes a couple of technical calls to individuals, checks the coxswains' steering and the two stroke rates, gives a shout for the last twenty strokes, and checks the times and margin.

The first piece is very close for a minute, and then the Empacher starts to edge out. They are nearly a length up by the end. There is a moderate west wind blowing down the course so the second piece, into the wind, takes a full minute longer and the margin increases.

Harry points out to me that the bow three and the five-seat in the Pocock are relatively weak. He tells the coxswains to pull the boats together, so the oars from each boat are pulled right across the gunnels of the other boat, and each rower sits right next to his equivalent seat in the other crew. The five-seats are told to switch places. They untie their shoes, climb across the small gap between gunnels, and settle into their new seats. The boats push away from one another, spin, and line up again heading downstream.

In the third piece the crews are nearly level for almost five minutes. "Well, we evened them out," says Harry. And this is what he wants: two matched crews, neither of which can beat the other easily; several minutes of tough competition when each rower and each coxswain tries to go faster, within the limits of the prescribed stroke-rate. Six minutes at twenty-six is intense enough work that it feels like real racing, but not so hard that they can't turn the boat around and do it all again after a few minutes' rest.

In the last five hundred meters, the Empacher is moving ahead slowly. Harry holds the launch behind and halfway between the wakes of the two crews, where it pitches gently from side to side. As the battling crews near the end, he calls to them: "Be patient . . . Nobody get anxious . . . Stay strong!" The Empacher has the momentum and takes another half-length in the last thirty strokes.

Heading upstream again, in the fourth piece, the Empacher moves out in the first two minutes. They have almost broken clear when Harry yells to the rowers in the Pocock. "Don't let them get away! Keep the pressure on! Be persistent!"

He pulls the launch a little farther ahead, directly behind the Empacher, and points the megaphone sideways, toward the Pocock. "Good! Keep the pressure on! Stay with them!"

They do. The bow of the Pocock stays overlapped with the stern of the Empacher as they approach Mass. Ave. Harry steers the launch back and forth behind the Pocock, focused only on them, his gravelly voice loud and slightly lower than usual, exhorting them: "Be perrr-sisss-tennnt!"

The stroke of the Pocock is a small, feisty racer. He gasps, and looks for the other crew. Since he is almost a full boat-length behind the Empacher's stern, he has to turn almost completely around to see them. With this kind of separation between crews, the bow pair may see the other crew's stern deck in their periphery, but the rest will only see the discouraging, roiling water of their puddles off to the left. They are racing an opponent they can't see. Harry: "Good! Dig in! Stay strong!" Someone growls. They hang on.

In the last twenty strokes the Pocock comes back by a couple of seats, but they have taken the rating up, consciously or not.

Harry is pleased. He tells both crews separately that it was "a good, solid piece of rowing." Good persistence, he tells them.

They paddle past BU and around the corner, and set up for one last piece up the Powerhouse Stretch, four minutes at twenty-eight this time, shorter but higher than the other four pieces. The twins stroking the Empacher stay a beat low, but the small stroke of the Pocock goes a beat too high and his boat takes half a length in the first part of the piece. Harry calls them down, and the twins draw back. The crews finish dead level.

———

Two days later Bill is taking two crews out in the cold, late afternoon of a snowy day, but Harry's squad are on the ergs, doing a 5k test. It has been almost two months since their last, though they were encouraged to try one on their own in January.

As in December, Harry talks to them in the final minutes as they warm up, looking from rower to rower, nodding as he talks. The rowers are talking to each other, but one will look up and nod back if Harry's gaze falls on him. "Find a good rhythm, a good pace. Be conservative. Find something you feel you can hold consistently, find where you are *today*. If you feel you can't hold it, back off. Good press with the legs, hold all the way to the finish."

During the piece: "Good persistence. Keep bearing down. Stay strong. Stay strong." Later that night, he sends the team an e-mail: "Outstanding! Great effort on the 5k pieces today!"

This is a strange time of year, the transition from winter training to the spring season, with many unknowns: Is training indoors or outdoors? Which will be more useful, a controllable session on the ergs, where individual efforts are visible and measurable, or a cold row in the boat, improving bladework, group cohesion, and racing skills? Which is more important for the team right now?

Harry, in a very unusual step, had individual meetings with each member of his squad back in December, to discuss their training goals for the winter. They were both surprised and intimidated by these one-on-ones with Harry, but they added some bite to the holiday points contest and to all their individual efforts. Harry knows he does not have the strength he has relied on for the last few years.

This week all the Newell squads have squeezed in some good rows on the open river, all the way through Saturday morning. But by the following Monday the river has frozen over again, with a discouragingly solid look, and the rowers are back on the ergs and in the tanks. Charley has the varsity lights in the Old Tanks, and Linda has her freshmen doing short, hard pieces on the back row of ergs.

Across the erg room, Harry is talking to Bill about something. The ergs are loud, the music is louder, and you can't hear what they are saying. Harry does most of the talking, and combines a slow nod of the head—up, then down—with a pushing away of the hand, like he's telling someone to slow down or relax. He does this periodically, and Bill nods a lot, which is a good idea when you talk to Harry. He could be scolding Bill, or telling him something about the Red Sox, or explaining the afternoon schedule in the Old Tanks. It's impossible to know. All these would look the same from across the room, although if it is baseball he might smile.

Most of Bill's guys are doing lower-intensity erging, but one of his foreign recruits is doing a 5k test on his own. He is trying to beat the qualifying time for The Club, a listing of freshmen who meet benchmark times for erg tests of various lengths. Bill sits down next to him during the last few minutes and cheers him home, enthusiastically and loudly. "Very nice! Very nice! You're strong! You're strong! Excellent!" The young man can hardly stay upright when he finishes, but he manages a little pump of his fist. For his efforts, which indeed make the Club standard, he wins a nice Cambridge University rowing vest.

Harry's guys do some short warmup pieces at two-thirds pressure in the new tanks, where Wayne is supervising and videotaping, and then five two-minute pieces on the erg at their target 2k pace. The CRASH-Bs (the World Indoor Rowing Championships, run by a Boston-based group known as the Charles River All-Star Has-Beens) are only two weeks from now, and they have not done much work at race cadence. Harry doesn't offer much guidance or advice during these short pieces. They are close to maximum effort for two minutes, then a break for longer than that. Most of them are able to repeat the same speed for all five, but the last two are tough. The fatigue starts reaching a critical level earlier and earlier—on the first piece it may not hit until the last thirty seconds or so, but on the fifth it may come after only a few strokes—and many falter, losing a second or so on their five-hundred-meter splits. Harry watches from all sides, and says "Good job. Good rowing, guys."

———

A notice makes its annual appearance on the bulletin board: "7 weeks until Race Day #1." Twice a week, now, there are morning practices at 7:30, and the intensity is building—physically and emotionally.

The weather is predicted to be cold through Saturday, and the squad elects to wait until Sunday before rowing on the water. On both Monday and Tuesday they do several full-pressure, one-minute pieces on the erg. On Wednesday they do a practice 2k erg at 95 percent pressure (two seconds per five hundred meters slower than their target 2k pace), followed by ten thirty-stroke pieces in the Old Tanks, building from three-quarter pressure to full. On Thursday they have a day off, and then lighter practices on Friday and Saturday. The CRASH-Bs are on Sunday.

On that Wednesday, Charley's varsity lightweights are on the back row of ergs, doing an hour of steady-state as he stands behind them, watching and occasionally commenting. They have target paces for the steady-state, and every six minutes they do a short burst at race pace. Charley wants to make sure they keep reaching the correct body positions even as they take up the stroke-rate and intensity, so they do a series of pauses, at body-over and half-slide, either before or after the bursts.

Charley has a bunch of guys he thinks have potential: strong, growing, but needing technical improvement. He has not done a single erg test with the team all year, and has no plans to do so. The have done some ten-minute pieces, and he has "taken note mentally" of where they are, but there have been no posted lists of the team's erg times. This year the championship regattas are a week or so later than usual, and he wants to keep the aerobic training going as long as he can. The lightweight field is extremely tight every year, with the small margins between rival crews shifting weekly. The winner of early races may not be the winner of the Eastern Sprints, and the winner of the Sprints may be overtaken at the IRA three weeks later. If you're at top speed at the end of March, says Charley, you'll be in trouble later on. Right now he is mostly focused on getting them to row well together: "If you've got two Italian lightweight scullers and one goes 6:04 and the other goes 6:03, do you need to work on their strength, or on getting them to move the boat together?" If they're that strong, that particular part of the formula is in place, and the gains will come in getting them to move the boat more efficiently and effectively as a unit.

Charley Butt is, without any question, a remarkably good coach. But start talking about the effectiveness of coaching with Charley, and he will immediately point out that a successful coach first needs good athletes, and he has been lucky with the athletes delivered to him at Harvard. They are nearly always chasing for medals at the Sprints and the National Championships. In contrast to the more wide-ranging styles that Harry manages to blend together, Charley seems to strive for technical uniformity. The Harvard lightweights are precise and well drilled, both their blades and their bodies. "The best-rowing crews on the river," according to an English observer who knew what he was talking about.

For more than a decade, Charley's varsity had the weirdest streak in the collegiate rowing world: They were national champions every *other* year. College lightweight racing tends to be a more closely shaved game than on the heavyweight side: The first races of the spring, between crews that have not faced each other all year, might have margins of half a second out of six minutes. The wide-angle perspective on training and tuning that Charley just expressed is typical for him. His crew may indeed lose a race or two, and lose the Sprints by a second, and then, over the next three weeks, Charley will make them better. He can tweak and peak his crews as well as anyone.

The other thing that will happen if you ask Charley about coaching is that he will tell you a story. It will illustrate some point, not necessarily one you were talking about, but a good one nonetheless. He may slap his thigh in glee, like a cowboy. He gets very excited about a racing story, and the key insight it reveals about a sculler's race plan, or a crew's ability to trust their base speed and pull out a sprint in the last 250. He may (or may not) give you details of some bizarre experiment he is trying with his athletes: pulling them with ropes, taping rods across their backs, putting sponges under their feet. While Harry will emphasize a technical point over and over again with an oarsman, run a drill to practice it, yell and exhort, Charley might literally tie the man up to get his body in the right position.

For all his success, Charley gets remarkably little attention. He does his job, does extra coaching (from Olympic hopefuls to veteran Cambridge Boat Club scullers), and shuttles home frequently for his "other job," the family of five children at home—though he likes to point out that his coaching job is not really "work." He has been at Harvard for decades, but the articles are not usually written about him. They are written about Harry. Despite that shadow, and the fact that Harry runs Newell Boathouse, there is no detectable rivalry or tension. They are both students of rowing. Each operates out of his own messy desk at either end of the small coaches' office. They talk. They learn from each other.

— ◦ —

On Sunday, more than half of Harry's team compete at the CRASH-Bs, and the rest do a 2k test at the boathouse. Maybe three-quarters of the team get personal best times. Three of the top ten college times at the championships are Harvard heavyweights, including the bronze medal, with a time of 6:00.9. The fastest eight times on the squad average under 6:06. Harry's e-mail on Monday says it was an "outstanding performance" by the squad. "WELL DONE!!"

Tuesday is another gray day, and by the time the two 3:15 p.m. crews put their boats in the water, it is forty degrees and raining. The coxswains are wearing new full-body storm-weather suits, but the rowers aren't unified in their gear choices. Some have tights, some are bare-legged; some have pogies on their hands, some have fingers exposed to the water and light wind.

Harry is wearing blue rubber-coated gloves that look like chemical-safety gloves—it's hard to keep out the rain with normal "waterproof" gear. He keeps the crews moving, doing tens by sixes, then twenties all eight, and laments the wind blowing straight into his face while heading downstream. A couple of times the launch knifes through small slushy ice floes. "Gives you an idea of the water temperature," says Harry.

He makes a few technical calls on the way down. There is a freshman in one boat, and his blade goes too high in the air as he slides toward the catch. Behind him, another rower's blade is hovering on the square, and Harry tells him to "start moving the blade to the water as you square it." There is some urgency in his voice. "Now's the time to decide to make that change!" he adds. Racing season is approaching.

The two eights line up at the finish line in the basin, and they do two pieces up and down the 2k racecourse. On Harry's command they start from the catch, do five strokes at three-quarter-slide, then ten strokes at thirty-two before settling down to twenty-eight, a profile that approximates the start of a race (though at lower cadences). Below Mass. Ave. there are a few sailboats tacking slowly in the middle of the river, and the crews have to steer around them slightly. One crew wins the first piece by a few lengths, and everyone looks cold. Harry comments in the launch that "we're probably warmer than they are." He tells the rowers to keep their hands warm, and calls Wayne on the cell phone to make sure the later group all wear pogies when they launch.

In the second piece the slower crew holds level for a minute or so, and then starts to slip back. Once again, Harry focuses on the trailing crew. "Keep the pressure on! Stay strong!" And once again, they manage to hold contact, hold a few seats of overlap. Just past the bridge he yells, "That's the way to hold them! That's the way to hold them! Now bring them back! Keep digging!"

By "digging," Harry does not mean oars-into-water, but mental digging, physiological digging, the constant quest to tap more internal resources and pour them out through the legs and onto the oar handle. The other crew is a benchmark, a challenge to be met, an opportunity to see how hard you can go, how much faster you can make your boat go. Be stubborn. Keep digging.

After the second piece ("good tough racing," Harry tells them), the crews paddle up to the BU bridge and stop underneath it, out of the rain for a few minutes. There are no other crews visible on the river. The raindrops are getting thicker.

On the way home Harry runs them through five bursts, building the pressure over five strokes, then twenty at full pressure. The first two are at thirty-two, then he has them try thirty-four for the last three. It's the first time they have gone above thirty-two this spring, and it's a bit rough: As they move more quickly, there's less time at the turning points of the stroke to maneuver the blade up and down, in and out of the water, so their accuracy suffers. Looking down the line of oars, the blades do not enter the water together, and some slip out of the water early, flicking up chunks of water as the bottom of the blade keeps moving and the rower feathers the oar. Harry tells them to make sure they hold the pressure right to the end of the stroke, so the blades stay covered. "Don't tear the blade out of the water," he says.

Halfway up the Powerhouse Stretch, the rain has turned to snow.

Scott Henderson '95

Harry coached the squad not so much by what he said but by what he didn't say. It has been mentioned by many that he was a man of few words. Although he was often cheerful around the boathouse and would joke with the squad from time to time, when it came to the rowing Harry was all business. He could be uncomfortably quiet in his launch during practice, standing behind us during erg tests or in the boat bays right before a race. It was almost impossible to know where you stood in the team's pecking order because Harry shared nothing. He rarely complimented rowers on their individual achievements, preferring to address the team as a whole. If I am honest, I frequently wondered what was going on in Harry's head: Did he think I had any innate talent, was he disappointed in my training, would he cut me from the varsity?

When Harry did share his thoughts, of course, we hung on his every word. Pre-race speeches were short on platitudes and long on seemingly mundane observations about the wind or boat speed—"Remember, crews tend to be a little faster around the thousand-meter mark." After a minute-long huddle in the boat bay, Harry would then abruptly turn around and walk away. I believe he cut these pre-race meetings short precisely because he did not want us to overthink the task at hand. Instead, he wanted us to stay relaxed, have faith in our preparation and believe that we were capable of exceeding what we thought were our physical and mental limits. Less was more.

Harry's genius was that he never tried to over-coach, let alone parent us. Instead, he let each oarsman decide for himself how much he wanted to commit to rowing. I don't remember him ever pressuring anyone who didn't want to make that commitment. For some, it was incompatible with their other pursuits, be it academic, social, etc., but that commitment was absolutely necessary in order to be successful in the program. In turn, Harry was prepared to use all means at his disposal to help us be successful. A critical part of our training was of course, physical conditioning. Harry also focused on our rowing technique, to the extent necessary to be competitive at that level. But he did not focus on it too much. Somewhat worryingly, we rarely practiced race starts leading up to races. I think

Harry believed that when all was said and done, races were won or lost not based on who rowed the prettiest, but who wanted it more. He would prepare us physically for competition, but ultimately it was our character, our mental toughness that would drive us over the finish line first.

I think of Harvard Crew often, but especially when I am facing a professional or personal challenge. I use my experience rowing under Harry as a kind of benchmark for judging the difficulty level of other things in my life. There have been few, if any, other times in my life when I worked as hard or was as thoroughly committed to one thing as Harvard Crew. I certainly have never been as physically strong nor have I experienced the kind of thrill and sense of accomplishment that comes with winning an important race such as the Harvard-Yale Regatta. Frankly, my four years as a Harvard oarsman give me the confidence and strength of mind to accomplish everything I have done in my life since graduation.

CHAPTER 6—MARCH

On This One

For several years the canonical way to imitate Harry Parker's voice was a sort of gruff sing-song. With a deep tone, sometimes with the throat slightly restricted, the official contour of every sentence was flat, then slightly down, then gradually up to a peak, then down to finish the last syllable or two. You would hear it when the rowers bantered with each other, when alums told stories, and during the nightly skits at Red Top (the training quarters where Harvard prepares for the Race against Yale), when someone took the role of Harry for the week. This standard Voice was passed down and adopted, immediately recognizable as HP. The best thing about it was that it did not sound like Harry.

There is the deep bass, used in a quiet room, almost monotone but with the occasional word emphasized. Sometimes a long sentence fades out, so you lean in to catch the last few words. There is the barking tenor, used in the megaphone, typically a few words at a time: a name, a comment, and a quick fix. There is the happy cheerleader, exclamatory and perky, used with recruits, high school campers, and anyone who needs to be impressed. There is the growl, used during competitive pieces: a single phrase, a single word, repeated two or three times, with two exclamation points to drive the point home, to plant these phrases in the rowers' heads. Drive it through!! Stay strong!!

Despite what everyone has said about him for more than forty years, Harry says a lot to his rowers. The appealing myth, perpetuated by reporters, authors, other coaches, and even his own athletes, is that Harry hardly ever says anything. When words do come, they are prized and scrutinized. "The Alan Greenspan of rowing," according to one. Yet Ted Washburn '65, coxswain and longtime fellow coach, says "it would never have occurred to me" to describe Harry as a silent coach. In contrast, he is "very active," but with the gift of being "comfortable in silence, letting a boat row."

It is the first week of March. The notice on the board now says "7̶ 6̶ 5 weeks until race day #1." Harry leaves his original piece of paper on the board, crosses out each number, and squeezes in the new one next to it with a Sharpie.

Two eights do some very close racing on Monday afternoon, three-minute pieces, always finishing within a few seats of each other. Harry loves it. At 7:30 Tuesday morning he walks into the lounge to talk to the whole squad. He tells them that when they sign up for practice they should indicate when they are actually available, not just times that he has typically scheduled crews. (One year he informed the team that "in case you didn't know it, your day belongs to me.") He specifically wants to get crews on the water earlier if possible: 4:15 is becoming a time when "you practically can't do any work" on the river, because of all the other crews out there. MIT is finally on the water, and BU, and Northeastern, and the high schools are starting up too. If we can't get out before then, he says, we're better off rowing after 5:00.

He reads off the crews from his list, muttering that he hopes he gets it right. There are three eights and a four scribbled on his paper, and he has shuffled crews slightly from the day before. He stands with the paper held just above waist height, head bent over it, and reads in a low voice. As he progresses through each crew list his voice loses volume, and the last few names are almost inaudible. It is a scene easily parodied in a Red Top skit.

It's windy but warm today, the warmest day since Florida. Wayne Berger takes the four on its own, and Harry follows the three eights upstream. Pulling away from the dock, Harry sees two hawks overhead. "Look at those hawks," he says. "Awesome." He takes out his cell phone and calls Wayne, who is not far upstream. "Look at the hawks circling above me!"

If not for the wind, Harry would have had the eights do two ten-minute pieces at twenty-six, but instead he opts for a lower intensity. Once they have warmed up he just tells them to go to three-quarter power, and they head all the way to the top of the rowable river by the Newton Yacht Club, where four large pleasure boats sit wrapped in white plastic at the deserted docks. There is a wide open stretch of water here, and today it is rough. Harry says the southwest wind would normally be blocked by the trees and leave this water calm, but now there are no leaves.

They turn, row two bridges downstream, about eight minutes at three-quarter pressure, come back up to the top, then down again all the way to Eliot—five minutes longer than before—before finally paddling home. On the upstream pieces there is a headwind, and Harry tells them repeatedly how to deal with the conditions: square the blade up late to get full compression before squaring, so the blade isn't being pushed back by the wind. When they turn he reminds them about the reversed wind direction and how to adjust their rowing. Spend more time on the slide, he says, and "don't get anxious" on the way forward.

Harry is getting impatient with his technical calls. One rower is over-reaching and he tells him to be "steady with the shoulders," not to hunch them over or reach more after reaching the front of the slide. "C'mon . . . change it!" he says. He still focuses mostly on the squaring and catch sequence. He tells another rower to "loosen your grip in the inside hand, square it later." The bow seat of one boat, the same one Harry switched last week between two eights, doesn't really get hold of the water. Harry tells him he needs to put the blade in before changing directions at the catch. In the launch he points out that this rower is strong—strong enough to be in the varsity. "But it depends on whether he figures this out . . . he's very wound up." He is tight in his hamstrings and calves, but also "wound up emotionally."

Crew selection is on everyone's mind. The small, tough Irishman and his close friends have often made guesses during the spring about the racing lineups. At this time last year, they got five out of eight correct for the varsity, and by spring break, before seat-racing, it was seven out of eight. They scrutinize the daily lineups, and especially the opposite seats when two crews go out together (since they are the most likely to be switched between boats in a seat-race), and who ends up in the stern fours.

They also try to guess the workout each day while they stretch in the lounge beforehand. There are some predictable patterns, or at least a set of possibilities, and a general sense that they will rotate between them. Before practice today, one of the varsity lightweights passes one of Harry's guys who was once a lightweight, and asks what they are doing today. The answer comes with a shrug and a smile: "probably hard pieces of some sort."

A couple of days later Harry has one eight on its own early in the afternoon. After the warmup, when they stop just below Weeks, Harry tells them they will do some twenties to warm up more, and then "some thirties, forties, and fifties" at rate thirty-four, so they get used to maintaining good bladework at the higher rate. The wind is nearly due west, and on many stretches of the river that means a direct headwind or tailwind and choppy water. They stay in the Powerhouse Stretch, doing two pieces in each direction and then spinning. On each lap they start from the catch, and do five strokes at two-thirds slide before lengthening out.

Once again, given the early start time, they are the only crew on the river for the first half of practice, and Harry relishes it. A Radcliffe four appears at one point and disappears into the Basin, and a few high school crews are launching from Riverside near the end of the session. The west side of the river is protected from the wind, and after the second trip downstream, Harry tells the coxswain that "as long as we're the only ones out here, let's go up the Boston arches." This is a complete violation of the normal traffic pattern, which on the Charles is as on the road: you must stay on the right-hand half of the river, which means the Cambridge side going upstream. Two laps later, the coxswain asks if he should still go up the Boston side, and Harry says yes, "we'll pretend it's our river."

Harry tells me he only recently realized that the Powerhouse Stretch is rowable when a west wind blows. The protection on the Boston side comes from buildings: a hotel, a biotech company, the newer additions to the Harvard Business School. But none of these was here when Harry first came to Boston. Back then a west wind would make the Powerhouse choppy and unpleasant, so he always took crews upstream from Newell in those conditions. If we had a few more buildings, he says, we'd have a great stretch of river here!

(The Powerhouse Stretch is so named because of the Blackstone Steam Plant, located near the top end of the straight, on the corner of Western Avenue and Memorial Drive. It was built in 1901 to run the new electric lighting in Cambridge, and started supplying steam to heat Harvard's buildings in 1930. The university now owns the facility, whose manager, Nick Peters, was not aware that his plant's identity has been invoked, however unknowingly, by the many thousands of rowers who have rowed up that kilometer of river.)

As it is the gusts are intermittent, and as the boats head roughly north or south the wind hits them from one side or the other, and feels like a headwind either way. It's another opportunity to practice headwind-style bladework, says Harry. "Keep the blades feathered until you are at full compression," he tells them. That way the wind can't slow them down.

The strong, "wound up" starboard is in the bow seat again, and for the most part Harry is happy with him. He seems to be Harry's "project" for the year, a strong but unstable oarsman who needs attention if he is to meet his own potential. Harry thinks he might make the varsity—he was in the "B" four at the Tail of the Charles in November, and is one of the strongest members of the squad. But his movements are a little stiff, his blade not always in time, not always taking hold of the water well enough. Harry puts him in the bow, and gives him a lot of attention.

But today it is the four-seat who gets most of Harry's coaching. His hands move away from the finish slowly, so his oar lags behind the other ports on the way forward, and then he has a sudden reach just before the catch, so his blade nearly catches up—but not quite. Mainly Harry talks to him about how he squares his blade. "You're making it harder for yourself," he says, "by squaring it too early. Leave it on the feather until the end, *then* square it just before the catch." On each piece, the four-seat's blade will start out in sync with the rest of the blades on his side, and then a few strokes later it starts squaring early, halfway through the recovery. "Loosen the grip with your thumb," Harry tells him. A tight grip with the inside hand, which controls the squaring, often leads to a slow turn of the handle. On every piece, every time they spin the boat, Harry talks to the four-seat about his blade. He tells two others their blades are rising too high off the water before they come down for the catch, and tells them to "reach out, rather than down." As he speaks, Harry's gloved left hand makes a little outwards swooping motion, mimicking the motion he wants to see.

"Some" pieces turns out to be: three thirties, two forties, two more thirties, a forty, a thirty, a forty, three more thirties, and one final forty. For the thirties the coxswain counts the strokes, but for the longer pieces Harry times a minute and fifteen seconds on his watch and calls out the moment to start counting the last ten strokes.

In his technical calls he focuses on the catch sequence, but reminds them often to be "solid in the water." For these pieces he says not to put a maximum effort into each stroke, but rather to focus on a solid push from the catch to the finish, to be consistent with this at the higher rate. After three laps he asks the four-seat how his bad knee is holding up, and the seven-seat about his back. All is well, so they keep going.

The oarsmen are clearly exhausted at the day's effort—intense work that adds up in time to more than three full 2,000-meter races—and they are visibly gasping after each piece on the last two laps. The very last piece is a "forty," and Harry almost forgets to call the last ten. A coach can lose track of time, and a coxswain will often lose count, but the rowers are aware of every stroke they take. That last piece was forty-four strokes, they say afterward. The others were forty-three.

With spring break two weeks away, many classes have midterms and papers coming due, so time is precious. One morning the rowers are sprawled around the lounge, stretching on the mat, sitting on the benches. One is perched on the bench-pull apparatus with sunlight bathing his shoulders through the large balcony window. Harry stands by the fireplace, rocking slowly from foot to foot as he talks to them. When they are pressed for time, the rowers will write "OYO" by their names when they sign up for a practice time, meaning "on your own"—they are opting out of the team practice. Harry asks the men to be judicious and only do this when necessary. But he adds that it is an acceptable option: "It is also understood on my end."

This morning they do longer pieces, the three eights chasing each other like a head race, at two-thirds pressure for a minute or so, then three-quarters, and then the last several minutes at 90 percent. BU to Eliot, Eliot to North Beacon, North Beacon to Eliot, and then a short paddle home. Harry stays close to the last of the three crews as they follow the other two up the river. The wind is westerly again but today a bit from the north, so there are no swirls from the buildings along the Powerhouse Stretch. But when they go through the Weeks footbridge and turn ninety degrees left, they emerge into a full headwind. Just as they do this, Harry tells them to increase the pressure from three-quarters to 90 percent. "Let's really get our teeth into it!!" he growls at them. As each coxswain crosses the designated finishing marker (the Belmont Hill School dock for the first piece, the downstream edge of the North Beacon Street Bridge for the second), she sticks a hand in the air for Harry to see, so he can mark times. But today he is not timing. "Perfectly conditioned," says Harry with a chuckle.

As they rest, waiting for the last piece heading downstream, the guys look tired. "Whaddaya say?" says Harry, before starting them off. Several minutes in, with a mile still to go, Harry encourages the third crew in line as he follows them: "That's good guys, stay focused, good relaxed recovery, good rhythm, moving well on the other two boats, moving well!" He has seen the gaps between the boats reduce slightly as the minutes tick by. "Good power each stroke! Keep the discipline! Good control!"

Heading down the last stretch of this piece, below the Northeastern boathouse, Harry says he is still happy with the bow-man he has been eyeing for the varsity. He has said nothing to him during the row today: He has just watched his blade, and it has behaved well.

The next afternoon the wind is southwesterly, and though the day was comfortable enough while the sun shone, by 3:00 the clouds have hidden it and the wind is biting. Harry takes the first crew downstream, warming up to thirty strokes per minute. While they are rowing by fours, Harry sees a couple of blades feathering in a way he doesn't like. "Don't *flip* the blade when you feather it, so your wrist goes down," he says; "just turn it." While the stern four rows he tells them to feather the blade with just the fingers of the inside hand, and keep their wrists flat above the handle the whole time. After twenty strokes or so he is satisfied, and they turn and head downstream by sixes.

When they reach the BU Bridge they turn, and Harry tells them they are doing a four-mile piece at twenty-eight strokes per minute. Some of them smile ruefully as they take off a layer of clothing and start to gird themselves. It's a long piece—twenty minutes of hard work—and they had no idea it was coming.

In fact, they never know what is coming. They can often guess the general style of workout—high or low intensity, long or short pieces—and they make predictions among themselves in the lounge before practice. But apart from seat-racing, and Basin pieces on Saturday morning, Harry doesn't tell them what the workout is until they finish warming up. Today, Harry himself didn't decide until they got downstream, and he says that is not unusual. He was thinking about two three-mile pieces, but when he saw the flat water and the lack of other crews on the river, he decided on the four-miler. It is not a workout they do often, partly because of river traffic, but partly because when water-time is limited, Harry likes to focus on other kinds of work. The later groups today probably won't do the four-mile piece, since by 4:15 the river will be full of other crews and it will be hard to do a long piece without being interrupted.

They do one final twenty upstream, then build up to twenty-eight at Riverside Boat Club. The four-miler takes them all the way to North Beacon Street, and they pass exactly one other crew, their own teammates in a four with Wayne coaching them. Harry is still reveling in this early-afternoon luxury, but knows it will end soon when the private schools come back from their spring break.

Every minute or so Harry raises the megaphone and urges them on. Mostly it is positive ("Well done! . . . Good pace, good bladework!"), but he has some comments for a few of them. Today a big rower in the four-seat gets special attention. He tends to speed up as he approaches the catch, and he puts his blade in early. Harry tells him over and over that he has to slow down, both during the warmup and then during the piece. The four-seat shakes his head a lot, stymied and frustrated. When he does manage to slow down, he ends up slightly too short, and his blade wavers in mid-air, rather than moving down and getting buried in the water. And then Harry gets on him about this, instead. Meanwhile, the two-seat is the oarsman with the bad knee from last week, and he is still struggling to feather and square his blade when Harry wants him to. Harry says, "two and four aren't really working together today." But he is happy with the starboard side today, and mostly lets them be.

After the four-miler upstream they do a second piece of just over a mile and a half, from North Beacon to just above Eliot Bridge. The southwest wind gave them a tailwind most of the way upstream, so now they row home in a headwind, and it is cold. Halfway through, blades are faltering in the wind, and the crew looks tired and disjointed. As they line up for the final straight shot after the Northeastern boathouse Harry says, "alright, just about three minutes to go—let's take it up to thirty . . . higher and stronger!" As they start to push for this final stretch, the focus seems to bring the crew together. Two minutes later Harry calls it up again to thirty-two for the final minute. And again they rise to it: faces are set with determination, legs and bodies moving deliberately and forcefully. It looks like they enjoy the challenge of going faster despite the fatigue. The stern pair mutter enthusiastically to the coxswain. When they stop, someone in the boat says, "awesome."

✦

Two weeks before the first race, Harvard's spring break begins. They have seat-raced a couple of times per week since the middle of March, on days when Harry can arrange two even eights. But this week he can schedule whomever he wants, whenever he wants, and there will be a lot of racing. Last week there was some hard work—two-minute pieces at full pressure—but also some more two- or three-milers at twenty-eight. Friday was low-key, the calm before the storm, and then on Saturday the racing begins. Harry sets up two groups, one practicing at 7:30 a.m. and 2:30 p.m., the other at 11:00 a.m. and 5:00 p.m. The earlier group is two fours, apparently racing for spots in the varsity eight. The later group is racing in eights to determine the second and third boats. Wayne joins Harry in the launch and they watch the races together, keeping track of margins, watching the rowers, talking about who to switch next. Wayne takes some video during the pieces.

The process known as "seat-racing" did not exist until the late 1960s, but it is now the ubiquitous standard, the way the rowing world assumes that athletes will be compared to each other and crews will be selected. It is as basic to the sport as the sliding seat, and Harry invented it. Or, at the very least, developed what are now the basic parameters: two roughly equal crews repeating the identical pieces of work, with a single swap of rowers in between pieces. Any change of margins should reflect the difference between just those two rowers.

Harry used this system to select the US national team crews in 1972, and the following year he wrote an explanatory note in *Oarsman* magazine. While traditionally a coach might have run time-trials with different versions of a full lineup, Harry posited that the rowers would feel more empowered, more in control of their own fate, if they are compared individually. Racing in any size boat is possible, he suggested, but since one man has less of an effect on an eight, and not all the rowers will be equally skillful in a pair, using fours is a "reasonable compromise." He laid out the reasoning behind the three-minute piece—long enough to test endurance, but not too long to be unrepeatable—but warned that the coach may overrule the result of the race if he suspects the "beaten" man will be a "better bet" over the longer 2,000 meters. Harry also allowed that the other rowers in the boat may not be consistent cogs from one piece to the next, thus eliminating any confidence that the comparison is a pure one, and that the "somewhat more acute distress encountered at racing cadence" should be taken into account.

In those days Harry was still a young legend. His Harvard crews were unbeaten for several years, and he had been given the reins of the national program. What was the wizard up to? How did he do it? In a reply to Harry's article, coach (and Olympian) Emory Clark declared that his "great respect for coach Parker was still intact and so was his secret." Considering all the variables that must be weighed in addition to the measurable race margins, Clark advised the oarsman who is being seat-raced to "kiss your momentarily inflated sense of control good-bye." Harry's article confirmed for Clark that ultimately, "coaches liken themselves unto the Deity and do exactly what they bloody well please."

As spring break begins, the Harvard squad seat-race in the first of the Saturday practices, twice on Sunday, and then both Monday and Tuesday mornings. The fours do six three-minute pieces Sunday morning: two races with the same lineup before switching men between crews, and then four more races in the afternoon.

On Monday morning Harry greets the eights group in the lounge and compliments them on the music playing in the erg room. It is country-western, which Harry says he can stand for longer than the techno and club mixes that often blast during erg sessions. He also has two things to say about the seat-racing. The first is that it is important to really focus on good rowing during the race pieces, rather than just tearing wildly into each stroke. Pay attention to the rhythm of the boat during the first strokes of the piece, he says, and make sure the whole crew is rowing well together. The second remark is that the rowers should "exercise a little discretion in drawing conclusions" from the racing, "and in *spreading* those conclusions." He and Wayne have heard, third-hand, the outcomes of the seat-racing, reported incorrectly, "and we look at each other and say, 'Oh! We didn't know that was the result!'" Harry points out that the relative margins from different races are important, but they are not the whole story, and then notes with a chuckle that clearly the rowers understand this, since when an oarsman is disappointed in a result he will come and remind the coaches of the other factors in play. Sleep, stress, water conditions, equipment, the coxswain's steering, and other rowers' inconsistencies and attitudes, are all potential flaws in the "objective" system of man-for-man seat-racing. (Kiss your sense of control good-bye.)

On Monday the eights are doing five-minute seat-racing pieces. As the crews do their final clothing adjustments, drink water, and align the boats, Harry explains. "When we go off, we'll go off the paddle. Make sure you're building it carefully, setting the blades, getting a good pry, moving together. We'll go five short-of-full, ten full at thirty-four. We're gonna settle right to thirty, and we're gonna go for five minutes, five minutes at a thirty. Let's have good headwind rowing." He tells the strokes to watch each other as they paddle off level, to adjust cadence and pressure to keep level until they start the piece. They only paddle for a few strokes before Harry yells, "oooooooooon this one." It's the deep, extended "on" that you hear, lasting two or three full seconds. The words "this one" are lost as his voice dies down—he starts dropping the megaphone even as he says them.

During the first piece one crew "stole the start" by rating higher than the prescribed cadences. The other crew is at twenty-nine, a beat low. "Not the sign of a good stroke," Harry chuckles. He yells to the high-rating stroke: "just a little high . . . give it a little more time." Harry recalls another, small-ish rower he often puts in the stroke seat, and how he "always cheats a bit" on the rating. When Wayne replies that he would take offense at calling it "cheating," Harry says, "but that is the fact of the matter."

At two minutes in Harry says "good pressure, stay focused, stay strong," and checks rates with his stroke watch. These crews are nearly the same as the previous day's last lineups, but with the bow seats switched. Harry asks Wayne how they finished yesterday, since this race, compared with yesterday's last, is essentially a comparison between those bow-men. One minute later, the crew that was called down earlier has taken the rate back up a little, in response to the other crew moving on them. Harry notices. "That's a good response; that's what a stroke *should* do." Wayne agrees, and suggests that this stroke could a good two-man for the JV. Harry counters that he would be a good stroke for the third boat, if that's where he ends up in the ranking. "One minute!" he calls out. The boats finish with a few seats of overlap. The coaches think they have learned what they need to about the bow-men. Harry decides to switch the five-seats.

"Well done, good rowing, really well done, guys. Very nice rowing." As the boats start to approach each other gradually, he says, "Careful, catch the blades, careful. You've gotta synchronize when you weigh enough." Harry micromanages the whole switching operation: where coxswains should aim (or "point") their bows as they approach each other, when each crew drops out some rowers to slow down, how many more strokes to take, when the rowers should grab each other's blades and pull across. He tells them to be careful as they climb across between boats. He seems not to trust them to pull this off without mishap.

Some coaches reduce seat-racing pieces to silent, precise exercises. The coach watches and takes note of times, stroke-rates, and margins. The coxswains are forbidden to motivate and drive the rowers; they simply steer straight and inform the crew of the stroke-rate and the passage of time. Harry knows that others do it this way, and agrees that "it can work." But these Harvard crews are really racing each other. The coxswains call power moves within the piece, Harry himself yells at the rowers, and they are totally invested in each outcome. It is not just selection. It is race training.

In the middle of the next piece: "that's good, feel the boat, nobody rushing, good compression, drive it through. That's two minutes. Keep digging, be stubborn. Good persistence now. Poise and power, poise and power." One crew pulls ahead, the other holds, then starts coming back. "That's good, hold the cadences steady. A minute and a half to go." The five-man who seems to be winning is a sophomore, who had come to Harry's summer youth rowing camp a couple of times, and sculled some after his freshman year, but hadn't raced much. Plus he spends his falls playing water polo, at which he excels. But he has a good rowing pedigree: Both his father and uncle were in Harvard crews of the early 1970s. "That's good, good poise, finish it out. That's good guys, that's really good rowing, really well done."

Downstream, as the boats recover and turn around near the Longfellow Bridge, Harry is thinking about bicycling. Some years ago on a cycling trip to Switzerland with some Harvard rowing alums, the group attempted the steepest climb around. The roads were narrow, the switchbacks tight. He was feeling good on that climb because he had managed to pull back and then "jump" one of the others, who he described as "a really good rider." Postal trucks have right of way on these roads, and one passed them coming around a tight bend. Harry was pinned against the side of the mountain, "hoping he wasn't going to crush me." Coming out of the situation intact, Harry was then delighted to see a sign for the Reichenbach Falls (where Sherlock Holmes died). Soon after came a lookout point where a set of binoculars were set up. They looked through to see rock climbers on their way up the face of the Eiger.

Before the fourth piece: "We've had a really solid row today, let's keep it up, let's finish the workout in just the same way, make sure *everybody* is focused on getting the boat moving, getting it up to speed strongly, settling into a really good rhythm, and then maintain the *rhythm* and the *power*." This time both strokes go off in unison, neither one giving up even one beat to the other.

First minute: "Good rhythm, feel the boat, drop in it, drive it through! . . . Set it in . . . ac*cel*erate!"

Second minute: "That's good. Now be strong! See how strong you can be!"

Third minute: "Two minutes gone . . . that's good. Stay focused. Good discipline, good rowing! Pay attention."

Fourth minute (to the trailing crew): "Bring 'em back! Dig your heels in, guys, dig your heels in!"

Near the end of the fourth minute, the crew that dropped back can feel their opponents slipping away. The men at bow, two, and three, who still overlap the other crew and see them off to the side, make little shouts of encouragement, and the entire crew responds. These men haven't been switched, and they probably think this is the last piece, so there is no personal gain to be had—they just want to win. The stroke-rate comes up slightly, they start to move, and the crews are nearly level when the five minutes are up. Wayne and Harry are impressed.

Now the coaches aren't sure what they want to do: They have done the switches they were interested in, but there is still time and space on the river to get some more work in. They decide to make one more switch, not because the outcome is vital, but because one of these rowers hasn't had the opportunity this spring, and the others have. They paddle upstream, past BU, and line the crews up at the bottom of the Powerhouse Stretch. One more piece, at a higher stroke-rate but shorter by more than a minute. "Dig in guys, be stubborn, stay strong. That's it, dig in, dig in."

Afterward Harry talks with both coxswains in the shop as they put away their cox-box equipment. He corrected both of them on their steering during the pieces today, and he now gives further advice on how to steer straight while next to another crew and while approaching the arch of a bridge. They also discuss how the different stroke-men respond to the start of a piece, some forcing the rate high initially, some holding back—the coxswains could make direct comparisons today since Harry switched the strokes between the crews today. These two coxswains are destined for the third and fourth eights, and those crews will be a re-seating of all of today's rowers.

⌒

The next morning, two fours are racing in the Powerhouse Stretch.

Readying for the first piece, Harry tells the coxswains where to point their bows ("I want you on the left side of the arch, close to the abutment"), and makes sure they are level. "Alright, five and ten at 34, then settle to 30 . . . Alright, let's sit ready . . . ready, go!" And a few seconds later, "Ooooooon this one!" There is a headwind from the southwest. As the crews settle Harry says, "Lengthen out, establish your rhythm. Set the blades in, and accelerate. Lean back into this wind!" He checks the stroke-rates during the piece; one crew is a little higher, and they take a lead of over a length. Harry and Wayne aren't sure what to do, and decide to just leave the crews as they are and race again upstream. The crews finish with half a length of overlap this time, and Wayne asks, "so do you just throw out the result of the first one?" and Harry nods. He says he always prefers to do two pieces between switches, and points out that the slower crew rowed the first piece out of the current and in low water near the shore (against his instructions), which probably slowed them.

Though he told them these races would be at rate thirty, in the first one both crews settle to thirty-two and Harry just lets them stay there. When they start the next piece, he tells them to row at the same rate as before. The start sequence is, build off the paddle to thirty-six for ten strokes, then settle to thirty-two for the remainder.

Twenty seconds into the first piece, Harry stops both crews: "It's thirty-six, not forty-one!" he yells at the strokes. On the restart, one crew takes a length of open water. With no switch for the second piece, they get the same result. The two-seats are swapped for the third piece, and the margins completely reverse: a full length advantage for the crew that had lost the first two pieces by open water. As they start to pull ahead, Harry points out that the man switched into the now-slower crew has good endurance, and says that "they might come back," but probably not until the last minute. He also notes that the other three men in that boat—two clear varsity members, and one of the twins—are mature racers, and will not be discouraged by an early deficit; they will keep going even though they are down. At about a minute to go, Harry starts exhorting both crews: stay strong, be persistent, keep the pressure on. The trailing crew stops the move and holds the margin to just about a length, bow slightly overlapping the other stern.

This change of margin is dramatic. This was conceived as a race to earn a place in the varsity, but the result now does more: It puts into question the loser's spot in the second boat. (And indeed, when lineups are named after this week, he is in the third boat.)

The bow-seats are switched for the fifth piece. The margin barely changes, though it might be slightly smaller. When they spin with no switching of oarsmen, there is probably four minutes of rest between the finish of one piece and the start of the next. Switching rowers between crews adds another four minutes. Eight minutes is a lot of rest, enough to repeat their performance without slowing down, but it gets progressively harder. One of the strokes looks spent at the end of the fourth race, grimacing as he leans forward, grasping the gunnel with his hands, sliding his seat forward and back to work the burn out of his legs. All the rowers are clearly fatigued as they line up for the sixth and final piece. Harry lets them know they can keep going. "Whaddaya say!" he exclaims. He tells them to keep the rowing strong when they're tired, but also to maintain their technique. "Power and poise," he reminds them.

Halfway through the last piece Harry looks up and sees that the slower crew has stopped the momentum of the faster one, and he starts nodding and saying, "yeah, that's it" before he even picks up the megaphone. He encourages them—"Yeah, draw them back! Keep on them, now!"—and for a moment it looks like they might start to reel in the leading crew, but in the end they have lost more ground than on the previous piece. The bow-men, it seems, are essentially equal.

A loon pops up between the two crews just after they weigh oars, and then disappears again underneath them. Harry lets the crews head home and spins the launch to try to get a look at the loon; he has seen it a few times recently but isn't quite sure what it is. He knows by the beak and the coloring that it is not a cormorant, but if it is a loon he thinks it is still immature. The loon surfaces and dives several more times as Harry circles toward it and Wayne tries to zoom in on it with his camera to get a better look. At one point the loon dives and Wayne pans his camera to the right in anticipation, but Harry points to the left, saying, "no, he'll come up over there," and he is right. Eventually satisfied, Harry heads in.

Back on the dock, two of the men who were just seat-raced ease themselves out of their respective boats, approach each other, and embrace. In the shop, standing by the workbench near the computer, Harry and Wayne review a list of starboard oarsmen, maybe half a dozen, with little to choose between them. One may end up in the first boat, but that leaves five, and Harry points out that one of them won't even make the JV.

As was intimated in the 1973 writings by Harry and Emory Clark, the margins of the seat-races are not the sole factor determining crew selection. Especially when the rankings are tight, it appears that Harry takes a "holistic approach," as one alumnus puts it. There are erg scores, of course, but also personality and group dynamics, individual psychology, and even the continuity of the squad: Sometimes it appeared that Harry might put a sophomore or two in the varsity to develop them and invest in the team's future. Such a decision might not change the speed of the current crews by much, but they weigh greatly on the minds of oarsmen whose confidence and self-worth might be bound up with earning a seat in a particular crew. Bitterness, even a sense of betrayal, are uncommon but not unknown among Harry's men.

This year, there are a couple more decisions to be made, and Harry expects to know his lineups by Friday. But he won't tell the team until the following Monday, after they have had the weekend off. They will have to wait.

On that Friday morning, Harry finds his coaching launch transformed into a tropical pirate party barge. Tiki lamps, a pink flamingo, and a black flag have been erected. A cocktail cup with umbrella is in the cup holder, and a hat labeled "Capt'n Harry" awaits him. Harry quietly removes some of the festoonery within a day, but the flamingo and flag stay in place for a full week. He has no idea who did it or why. He chuckles to himself, but never discusses it with the rowers.

Scott McMullin, MP '96

Harry definitely isn't a cheerleader and he doesn't make grand speeches to try and pump you up. I think what he really does to motivate both individuals and the team is that he makes them believe in themselves. Going in to a race we always felt like we had done all of the preparation and there were no doubts that we were ready to take up the challenge. One of his pre-race speeches to us went something along the lines of, "Have a good, clean catch, strong through the water, clean release, and then just come up the slide and do it again."

I have had coaches both before and after Harry. He was very distant and very quiet in comparison. He was there as a coach and not to be your best friend or cheerleader. He was also focused on the absolute fundamentals of rowing. He never forced anyone into any particular body position or stroke, but let them develop on their own through miles on the river.

He seems to have softened a little. I'm not sure what has caused this, be it Abigail, fast crews over the last several years, only seeing him once or twice a year, or maybe I've just matured some. Training has definitely changed. I recently became aware that there are no more uninterrupted Hours-of-Power or 22.5ks on the erg. There is an ice machine in the boathouse and yoga is encouraged! Unbelievable! I guess these are all good things and help to keep the kids healthy, and it also allows me to talk about "the old days" when we were tougher.

Matt Moeser '96

The one thing that stands out in my mind is that Harry never lost his cool. I know he was mad at me on more than one occasion but he never really blew his stack. I am sure he was disappointed sometimes with our results, and he might say something like, "Time to start finishing first," but he never got down on us.

Harry was really angry at me twice. In fall 1995, I ran a pair into a bridge which resulted in a long scolding involving such phrases as, "What were you thinking? Don't say anything . . . You weren't thinking! . . . That's not bad rowing, that's carelessness!" He got over that (eventually). The second time he got really angry at me was in spring 1996 after the Eastern Sprints. I had gotten into a physical altercation on the water after the heats with someone in my boat and was the aggressor and completely at fault. I don't know if he knew about it on Sunday or not. When I came down to the boathouse on Monday, he and I had a very stormy conversation that ultimately led to him kicking me off the team later that week. He told me to talk to and apologize to everyone in my boat, which I did. I don't really know if Harry made the decision or the people in the boat made the decision, but eventually he called me down to the boathouse and gave me the news. I cannot say he was wrong to do what he did. We shook hands and that was it. I think he sent me a letter with my letter sweater that summer and I wrote him back once or twice and I think e-mailed him once.

Harry was patient with me and with most people (from what I remember). He wanted me to row better and he never gave up on me. If there was any deficiency in my rowing, it was because of me and not because of his coaching. He never quit on me and I hope he never thought I quit on him.

CHAPTER 7—APRIL

Whaddaya Say

ON THE MONDAY AFTER SPRING BREAK, HARRY'S CREWS ROW IN THEIR racing lineups for the first time. The squad heard nothing during their weekend off, and when they got an e-mail summoning the team to a 7:10 a.m. practice on Monday, some had assumed there would be more seat-racing. But now, when Harry walks into the locker room, he tacks up a list of four eights and announces that these are the boatings that will race next weekend. The men are not shocked when they see the lineups. One or two in the second boat thought they had a shot at the first boat, and likewise at each cutoff between crews, so of course some are disappointed. And in a squad this deep, it is a tough reality check for those in the fourth boat, as well as for the few not named to any crew at all.

From now on, the varsity and JV will row with Harry, the third and fourth boats with Wayne. There will be some practices when all crews will be together, perhaps one or two every week. They may not even row at the same time, and indeed they are usually offset by half an hour on weekday mornings, which turns out to be the best time for most crews to guarantee full attendance.

The second boat is dominated by smaller men. The two in the very middle, four and five, are larger, but even the five-man, sitting in a traditionally larger rower's position, is slight of build. The four-man is the junior from last fall's Club Four, the one Harry said "doesn't like to train." He has stuck it out and done well, sitting in the "engine room" of a very good JV crew. The feisty, thin junior who has often led crews from the stroke seat has taken up that position in this boat, with a small, racy senior behind him at seven. These two form a smooth, tight stern pair. The Irishman is at bow, and both twins are in the boat, on either end of the engine room at three and six. The sometimes-spotty Serb with the bad knee is at two.

It seems that all the right people have ended up in the varsity. Last year's stroke, the Englishman, is there once again. The other members of the Championship Four from the fall are at seven, five, and four, all strong seniors, including the captain. (There had been talk in the squad about a "curse" on Harvard captains that kept them out of the first boat, after a few recent team captains ended up in the JV. But it was never likely for this year's captain, a likeable, sociable man who leads by example and is one of the better rowers; the "cursed" captains were generally weaker oarsmen, but had been elected by their teammates for their leadership and work ethic.) At two is another senior, one of the smoothest and most determined of the group. The six-man is a success story, a large junior who was in last year's third boat but made great progress this year. And the "wound up" junior, Harry's project this year, sailed through the selection process with a series of seat-racing victories that landed him in the bow seat of the Harvard varsity.

They row twice on Monday, doing a lot of short, hard pieces, trying out some "starts" at high ratings, then settling down into racing cadence. The captain says he isn't worried about the lack of high-rate work recently, since their stroke-man tends to start high anyway . . . and then stay high.

After a brief return to the academic world of Harvard College, the first and second boats fly to California on Thursday morning for the San Diego Crew Classic, a large regatta on the Redwood Shores featuring every imaginable boat class and age group. For many years this was Harvard's season opener, but when Harry decided to add a Florida trip to the winter training program, the trip to San Diego seemed like a large expense. After several years away, he has been enticed back. The Crew Classic is set up like a championship regatta: six boats side by side for each race, with heats on Saturday to qualify for the finals on Sunday. It is a taste of what next month will bring at the Eastern Sprints and the IRA regatta, including some of the same competition.

The JV take home the trophy in their event. They row the heat low at a thirty-three and let Washington pull ahead in the last five hundred meters, knowing that both crews will qualify for the final and get placed into favored lanes for that race. On Sunday Harvard takes the lead before the halfway mark and holds on for a two-second victory.

The varsity, despite the captain's confidence in their zippy start, gets dropped by Washington immediately in their Saturday heat. They work back into them in the body, but give away a five-second margin overall. In the final they squeeze out a bronze medal behind Washington and Princeton, a few seats ahead of Cal Berkeley and Northeastern. They come away feeling that their base speed is good, but they need to improve their start.

For the winning JV crew, the traditional shirt exchange is an amusing scene. It is a good way to start the season, having eleven crews come by to forfeit their racing gear into their hands. Some of the West Coast schools gave up tank-tops, a welcome novelty for those used to the T-shirts favored in the Northeast. But they will hang loose on the Harvard JV, who are dramatically smaller than the hulking oarsmen from Washington and Cal. Even the four-man, the largest in the crew, tilts his head upwards to meet the eyes of his Washington counterpart when shaking his hand and taking his shirt.

The Crew Classic has refocused Harry and the top two crews. Back in Cambridge, Monday's stormy weather keeps the crews indoors, where they work on technique in the tanks. Harry wants them to push their hands and bodies out earlier from the finish, and emphasize the swing of the back during the drive, generating a firmer finish. The next day they put this to practice during competitive pieces up and down the length of the Powerhouse Stretch. Harry is not in a talkative mood on this Tuesday. A high school prospect and a visitor from Australia are on board, and he says nothing to his guests during the whole practice. He gets frustrated with the coxswains ("You came too wide on the turn . . . you have to pay attention, we talked about that . . ."), and is focused on getting the day's work done without wasting time or getting caught behind other crews. He makes some comments on blade height, length, and reach (the four-seat of varsity looks too short: "Relax the shoulders, rotate them as you come into the catch"), but mostly he focuses on the speed away from finish, matching up their body swing, and holding the blade through to the finish during the drive, the same lessons as in the tanks yesterday.

These two crews have a new perspective on themselves and their competition. As they do warmup thirties next to each other, lining up level to start each one, a few men in each boat glance across, checking relative speeds, feeling the other crew shift forward or backward. Obviously the first boat is faster than the second—they were chosen to be so, from the same group of athletes—and they take nearly a length on every thirty-stroke piece. And yet they are competitors, and they have to look: the varsity stroke simply confirming that they are faster, the JV bow-man hoping to confound the established order by not being slower.

In the first four-minute piece, Harry starts the varsity half a boat-length behind the JV, and they finish nearly a length up. It is the same in the second and third pieces. The JV coxswain pushes them hard, tells them they are holding themselves to a higher standard, trying to match a varsity crew, not another second boat. They are pouring themselves into each piece, working much harder at rate twenty-eight than the varsity, who seem within themselves, slowly slipping ahead and just barely breaking free. After the third piece the second boat looks wasted, and on the fourth they drag, letting the varsity walk away with a length of open water. Harry notices the lapse and calls them out, and on the last piece they fight hard for the first two minutes, hardly letting the varsity take even a seat. The coxswain steers too far to the left, threatening to mow down an oncoming sculler, and as she makes a sudden steering correction the rudder drags, the boat's balance is upset, the focus and momentum are lost. They have four days to keep consolidating, before going head-to-head with Brown on Saturday.

THE STEIN CUP, APRIL 12

On Thursday morning Harry takes the varsity on their own for a technical row. It is a mild morning, warmer than in recent days, the sun just barely making an appearance, the water calm. Harry stands with them in the boat bay for a few minutes before they launch, talking quietly. He tells them they need to make sure they get sleep before the race with Brown this weekend, and that tonight is especially important.

Out on the water, the rowing matches the weather, relaxed and picturesque. Harry keeps them rowing by sixes for a while, doing pauses late in the slide, with the handle over the toes, just before squaring the blade. He is still trying to get a couple of them to sync up their sequence of motions away from the finish, so that all eight blades and bodies move out together. This pause position can be an awkward one, since the rower is crouched forward, knees bent, body-weight divided between the seat and the feet, and the blade in mid-air. By sixes, though, the boat is held stable by the blades of the two who are not rowing. After a few minutes they go back to rowing without the pause, then row all eight for the first time as they approach the BU Bridge; and then Harry tells the coxswain to call the pause again, with all eight rowing. It is nearly perfect: On each stroke all eight blades emerge from the water, feather to horizontal as they start to move back, glide through the air just a couple of inches above the still surface of the water, and then hover there as all eight bodies come to rest and balance, still and poised, for the moments of the pause. The discrepancies come after the cox says "go" and they move again toward the catch. Blades square up at slightly different times, a couple of them rising higher than necessary before coming down again to the water. Harry calls out the captain, rowing in the four-seat, whose blade doesn't swing back to the same angle as the others on the port side.

They row about six miles this morning, mostly at two-thirds pressure, with Harry making gentle comments every so often. He emphasizes "careful rowing," which means attention on technique rather than power. They do a couple of short bursts at three-quarters and 90 percent pressure near the end. After they turn and start paddling home, the captain's oar-angle has suddenly gotten much worse. Harry believes he was up half the night writing a paper, though when he repeats his comments back on shore about getting sleep, with a special stare at the captain, the man protests that in fact he got plenty of sleep last night.

The weather forecast for Saturday in Providence is forty degrees, a northeast wind against an incoming tide on the Seekonk River, and rain. It is completely wrong, except for the tide: The wind is southerly, the sun surprisingly strong, and the temperature seventy degrees. As Joe and Blocker do final checks of the boats, Wayne meets with the third and fourth boats, and Harry with the first and second. Brown's new boathouse is next to a park, and the curbs and landscaping are still being completed. The crews stand on the grass in the partial shade of still-leafless trees. Harry talks for about three minutes. He notes that the wind will be against them as they race south, so they should use the headwind technique they have practiced. He reminds them that Brown is one of the fastest teams in the country, and they should expect very fast starts from all crews. He suggests a ten-stroke push at around five hundred meters and a twenty at the halfway point. Keep the pressure on no matter where you are in the course, he says, and adds, "Don't be afraid to think nasty thoughts about the other crew." While he talks there is a sudden cheer of "Harvard!" from Wayne's crews across the parking lot, signaling the end of their meeting. Harry finishes ("let's have a good race"), claps his hands once, and they disperse.

Later, Wayne comments that the lack of drama in Harry's speeches is a reminder that real motivation has to be internal. He is almost universally remembered as *not* a cheerleader. Adam Holland '94, recalling the 1992 collegiate National Championship final, wrote that Harry's pre-race speech, "one of the most stirring, inspiring things I have ever heard, was simply, 'Guys, you've done the work. Go out there and revel in your prowess!'"

Harry, Bill, and Wayne follow the races from one of Brown's coaching launches. Harry drives. As they make their way upstream before the first of the freshman races, they feel for the wind, try to discern how it affects the water on different parts of the two-kilometer racecourse. Harry phones Joe back at the boathouse to convey some last-minute steering instructions to the varsity coxswains before they launch.

As the regatta progresses, Harvard is winning every race. Two Harvard freshman fours finish well ahead of Brown's four, and the freshman eight responds to an early Brown lead with a strong surge to win by almost a length. The third and fourth eights are closer to one another than they are to Brown's trailing third boat, and the Harvard JV wins by two lengths, never really threatened. All morning long, the headwind increases and the water gets choppier.

As the tide on the Seekonk reaches its peak, the first boats burst off the start in bouncy water. They remain nearly level for most of the first minute, then Brown pushes slightly ahead. Harvard stays with them, though, and in the second minute they draw back level, perhaps slightly ahead—it looks like the beginning of a classic Harvard middle thousand, where they simply move inexorably through their fast-starting opponent. This is what Bill's crew did about forty-five minutes ago, and now he intones, "c'mon boys" and "do it now." Both crews are struggling with the conditions. Blades and oar shafts get caught by swells, and bits of white spray leap across them. Harry speaks very quietly to himself: "Keep digging, keep pushing." But Harvard's move doesn't last. Halfway through the race Brown makes a huge push, their two-man yelling "Now!" as they start to move away from Harvard. Brown keeps moving away and before long, the race is essentially over. They win by five seconds.

Harry is quiet after the race ends. He brings the launch up behind his crew and waits. A few minutes later they start paddling by sixes toward the boathouse and Harry follows, staying slightly to the side. He says nothing, but glances over at them periodically. The rowers don't look at Harry as they row back to the boathouse. The stroke just drifts his blade through the water, half buried, looking down and grimacing. Others also look down, many of them with frowns or blank looks on their faces. When Harry moves the launch directly behind the crew, some of them now turn their heads to the side. As they go under the final bridge before the boathouse, Harry finally speaks. "Heads up as you head in now. Show some poise."

Later, when I ask if he is surprised by the result, Harry nods and says it was "a disappointment. They didn't handle the conditions well." As the Brown crews enjoy a barbecue with their families and supporters, Harvard de-rigs their boats and loads them back onto the trailer. Though all but one Harvard crew has beaten Brown, the Stein Cup goes to the winner of the varsity race. They hand over their shirts, along with the cup.

THE COMPTON CUP, APRIL 19

This week there are changes. Harry tells the squad that although he still thinks he had picked the eight strongest guys for the varsity, they weren't acting as a cohesive unit. The bow-man, his project this spring, is moved to the three-seat of the JV. In that boat, the twin at three moves to seven, right in front of his brother, and the small seven-man is promoted to the bow seat of the varsity. He is pleased—he knows he isn't as big or strong as the man he is replacing, but his technical prowess may help the varsity stabilize and gel.

Tuesday morning Harry's and Bill's crews do a few Basin pieces. It is a tough workout but it goes well. The JV has been given an increase of raw power, and if anything they get faster relative to the freshmen. Harry tells them it will be the only really hard work this week. That afternoon the varsity's new bow-man goes for a light row in a pair with the stroke of the crew, and the next day they are the new stern pair. Seven, five, and three all shift back one starboard seat, and six and four switch places. Wednesday morning is all pause-drills and long stretches at two-thirds pressure, getting the new lineup to take strokes as a unit, think about them, adjust to the new feel of the crew.

The weather is perfect this week, at least through Thursday. Harry jokes about getting used to the good conditions, but adds seriously that in fact, the weather was a factor at the Brown race. Though they have rowed in some wind, they have mostly avoided rough water this spring, and their inability to handle it was their downfall. This may be especially true of the now-demoted bow-man, and Harry says the worry with him was always that you didn't know if his technique would hold together under pressure. The boat was stronger with him in it, but it was "riskier" to have him there. On Thursday morning, which is beautiful and warm with very little wind, the crews rehearse their pre-race warmup for the weekend, all the way down to the starting line in the basin. They get set on the line and do a single two-minute piece, just like the first third of a race, and then paddle the rest of the course. As they cross the finish line, Harry says to each crew, "Whaddaya say—let's get here first on Saturday!"

Which is what they do, eventually. These races between Harvard and Princeton are nearly always battles. Since there are three schools in the

Compton Cup, and two of them (Harvard and MIT) are from Boston, the race takes place on the Charles two out of every three years. Harvard nearly always beats Princeton when the race is here, even in years when Princeton is supposed to be faster. In one such year perhaps a decade ago, the Princeton coach made a little speech before handing the cup over to Harry on the MIT dock. He asked Harry, haven't you considered retiring? Is it about the money? The other coaches, he assured the crowd, would happily chip in for Abigail's college fund.

The morning has a similar feel to last week's session at Brown: solid victories across the board. The Harvard fourth eight and the second freshman eight both beat Princeton's third eight. A six-second victory for the freshmen, eight seconds for the JV.

Again the varsity faces a fierce start from their opponents, but this time the conditions are beautiful, with a tailwind building up to make the later race times fairly quick. Princeton immediately jumps out to nearly a half-length lead, and pushes another seat or two ahead in the first five hundred meters. Harvard has a shockingly bad start that keeps them closer to MIT than Princeton, and the coxswain steers them off point—every move of the rudder drags on the boat and disturbs its delicate balance. As they did against Brown, Harvard uses the second five hundred meters to push back into Princeton, gaining back seats one by one, shooting under Mass. Ave. only three seats down.

And then they push again. They gain by inches. Passing the MIT boathouse, with six hundred meters to go, they lift the stroke-rate to forty and sprint the rest of the way. Princeton, perhaps surprised (they did after all beat Harvard in San Diego only two weeks ago) and clearly out-raced on this day, can do nothing to respond. Harvard crosses the line 0.5 second ahead, a one-seat margin. It is a glorious race, a reassuring victory, a validation of the refocus and reshuffling of the past week. Harry smiles warmly.

On the same morning, Charley's lightweight varsity loses by 0.05 second after a gutsy sprint from Dartmouth, a photo finish with a judgment of less than one foot. In the face of condolences Charley is philosophical, which is normal for him when he isn't being funny. He has six sophomores in his first boat, he says, two of them walk-ons a year ago, and they are still learning how to race. He describes Dartmouth as "shaved and tapered," using a swimming analogy. The year before, Dartmouth won the Eastern Sprints. In this race Harvard had a good first thousand meters and by next week, says Charley, maybe they'll have a good fifteen hundred, and the week after, 1,750, and then maybe they can put together the whole package for the Sprints. He can only expect so much from them, he says, and it would be disastrous to get hung up on losing these races. He thinks the rest of the season will be "fun" and "interesting" to watch. Plus, Linda's freshmen are good, so the future is bright.

THE ADAMS CUP, APRIL 26

The next week has a familiar pattern: racing in the Basin on Tuesday morning, steady-state and drills on Wednesday. This week Harry keeps them working until Thursday, since their opponents this weekend, the Naval Academy and the University of Pennsylvania, do not appear as challenging as Brown and Princeton have been. On Wednesday they do some drills, spend time rowing by sixes, and then do several miles at two-thirds and three-quarter pressure. Thursday starts similarly with work by sixes, and then they do four ten-minute pieces between the Eliot and North Beacon Street bridges, building from two-thirds to three-quarters and finally 90 percent pressure. Harry sends the varsity first for two of the pieces, and the JV first for the other two, so he has time to watch each crew.

Harry's "project," now in the JV three-seat, is still getting a lot of attention. This week Harry tells him often that he is "too eager to pull," his blade not getting hold of the water as he starts to push his legs. Harry tells him to apply minimal pressure to the oar right after the catch, then increase it later, hoping he will get a feel for locking onto the water and pushing off it. Sometimes it is better, but more often now he draws the handle upwards, instead of horizontally backwards, as he starts the drive, and the blade goes deep into the water, burying half the oar shaft.

Meanwhile, the twin in the JV seven-seat is also drawing comments from Harry, as he squares his blade gradually, and never completely, during the recovery. Harry tells him he is gripping too tightly, and that he should square it later and more quickly, and make sure it squares completely before the catch. He comes back to him again and again about this during practices this week, and it never quite sticks. At one point, Harry quips that the three-man must be happy someone else is getting some of his attention.

For the second week in a row, Harry changes the lineup of the varsity eight. The personnel stay the same, but he re-rigs the boat to make a "bucket": The bow and two-man switch spots, so now both two and three are on the same side, and bow is the same side as four, rather than the usual alternation of port-starboard all the way down the boat. The "eccentric" or "German" rig was a novelty in the United States when Harry started using it in the 1960s. His original reason to use it, and the reason he is using it now, is for steering: It has been an issue all season, he says, especially during racing starts, that the varsity veers toward port. The start against Princeton was so bad he finally decided to try the bucket. The bow seat is now a port, and his blade, at the catch, will tend to pull the boat toward starboard. Harry's early crews in the mid-1960s had a bucket in the middle of the boat, with four and five both on starboard. It was so common in Harvard crews of that era that at one point, when Harry went to a standard rig one year, the man who moved out of the bucket from four to three said he didn't even know how to row without someone immediately in front of him on the same side. Harry has rowed with seven-six buckets, too. This year's captain declares with sarcastic glee that since the successful crews of 2005 and 2007 were both bucketed, his boat is now "guaranteed to be fast."

When Harry started coaching, he didn't know what to look for in his rowers. At Penn they had not had the sort of video analysis that is common today. There were films of rowing, "newsreels," but they couldn't pick apart technique in the same way. He had years of Joe Burk's coaching to draw on, though, and his own training diaries, which he could look at and find the sequences of "adjusting this, adjusting that" that marked his own progress through the sport. In the first couple of years, he realized some of what he was trying didn't work. He remembers a moment, seeing a photo of some crew at the finish of their stroke, and realizing, "*that's* what I want." So he made a change, and his crews got better.

He keeps records of the team's daily work, and consults them. He writes it down after the fact, since each day's workout isn't set out precisely beforehand. Harry doesn't follow a rigid training regimen. He doesn't follow "macrocycles," or a schedule of hard weeks and easy weeks, or calculate what percentage of the training is aerobic versus anaerobic. There may be an ideal regimen for rowing, he says, but the evidence shows that various methods work. Clearly, Harry's method works. He has a general framework for the year, and a range of different kinds of workouts he wants to get in each week. They can't always get everything in, especially if there is a race to taper for. He recognizes that their steady-state is probably at too low an intensity for the ideal training effect, but "that's why we do the building pieces."

⚊ ⚊

If you walk around the boathouse of the University of Pennsylvania, where Harry Parker began his career in rowing, you could easily miss his presence. There are three photos, all featuring the 1955 crew that won Henley, and two of these photos are identical.

The Penn varsity are rowing in a shell named after Joe Burk, who died in January and was Harry's coach for nearly his entire rowing career. When Harry started at Penn, he was a lightweight. The lightweight coaching position was unfilled when the year started, and it was Burk who taught the freshman lightweights to row, first in the rowing tanks and then on the water. Eventually they hired a British graduate student named John Blacker. Harry still sees Blacker on occasion at Henley, and this recollection makes him smile. Blacker was a good coach, says Harry, and unlike many other coaches, "he told us about the lore of rowing."

The lore of Harvard rowing now includes the name Dick Cashin, and whether they know this lore or not, the men of Newell Boathouse are in Cashin's photographic presence every day. His face looks out from the enormous picture in the main stairwell. He is in the six-seat of the famous "Rude and Smooth" crew, hunched a little, intent and furious. Cashin's freshman photo in the locker room is eleven years later than, and about eleven feet to the right of, Ted Washburn's. In the same class as Cashin was Tiff Wood, one of the scullers immortalized in David Halberstam's *The Amateurs*. Both Cashin and Wood have sons starting at Harvard this year, and they are rowing, but their crew picture may not appear in this room with their fathers: They are both in the *second* freshman boat, and only first-boat photos are hung. The occasional exception is for undefeated second boats, and so far this spring Cashin and Wood have not lost a race.

Dick Cashin runs a major equity firm. He hires former rowers to work with him. In addition to his Harvard and US national team successes, he holds an indoor rowing world record for the fifty-plus age group. On his birthday every year, he cycles the number of miles that matches his age. He has dinner with the mayor of New York City, and refers to him with a nickname. He has remained very close to Harry over the years, and specifically mentioned him in his message to classmates on the occasion of their twenty-fifth reunion.

Joining the coaches in a launch to watch the racing in Philadelphia, Cashin sits directly behind Harry while Bill drives. Cashin bicycles and golfs with Harry. They went golfing with a group of Harvard rowing alums the previous weekend, and Cashin asks if Harry was driving the ball well. Harry was having some shoulder pain, and when Cashin asks where he felt it, he reaches his hands around Harry and prods his shoulders. In the context of Harry's interactions with most other people, this is an act of astonishing familiarity. (The night before, at dinner, the varsity four-man told Harry he had seen a photo of his 1955 Henley crew in the Penn boathouse. He joked that it looked like Harry was missing water at the catch. This was a fib, since the photo was a posed team photo, not an action shot, but Harry was not amused. Later a teammate told the four-man that he had "crossed the line.")

Harry's cap flies off in the wind, and he drives the launch back to retrieve it. The cap reads MT. WASHINGTON CENTURY on the front. Cashin explains that there is a one-hundred-mile bike ride every year, the day after the race up Mount Washington. Cashin and a couple of others joined Harry for the hill-climb for a few years, but they didn't learn of the century ride until later. "Thank God Harry didn't know about it then," says Cashin.

Harry's lineup shuffle in the varsity does the trick. Once again, every Harvard crew wins this morning: the 2F by eight seconds, the 1F by fifteen, after the Navy seven-man is "ejected" from the boat by his own oar handle when his blade gets caught in the water. (He is picked up by one of the following coaching launches, and Bill yells out, "hold your head high—it means you were pulling hard.") The JV finish their race nearly twenty seconds before Navy, sliding out to an early lead and then driving the point home with a deliberate surge at the thousand. In the varsity race, the first minute is a little uncertain, since the starting line is staggered in Philadelphia, to balance out a starboard turn six hundred meters into the race. But soon it is clear that Harvard is leading. By the halfway mark they have open water on both Navy and Penn, and though Navy mounts a solid sprint coming down Peters Island, Harvard finishes a full length ahead.

This is neither a surprising nor an unusual result in recent Adams Cup regattas—it is the ninth time in a row Harvard has won it. But if the contest has not been hotly contested in recent years it still holds a special meaning for Harry, given his connections to all three participants. Penn was where he started rowing, the Navy allowed him to train for the Olympics, and Harvard has been his home for almost fifty years.

One year not too long ago, after yet another home victory over Penn and Navy, Harry stood on the dock chatting with Bill, Kathy, and Abigail. He held the Adams Cup, examining in the morning sun the inscribed list of winners for each year, the last few decades almost exclusively "Harvard." This was the first big race he won when he rowed for Penn, he said. Navy had had a streak of several years. He turned the cup around to the 1950s and read: "Navy—nineteen fifty-two, fifty-three, fifty-four . . ." and then, with a little smile of satisfaction and a hint of a dramatic tone, "Pennsylvania!"

THE SMITH CUP, MAY 3

A breezy mid-week morning, four eights in the Basin: Harry's two eights, a third varsity with a shuffled lineup due to injury, and Bill's first boat. They do a full pre-race warmup, completing it at BU, pointing downstream toward Mass. Ave. Harry hovers at the finish line, aligns the crews, tells the coxswains which arches on the bridge to aim for ("the right side of the wide arch just to the right of the twin towers," or "the small arch under the gold dome," for example). Three crews start level, with the 3V half a length ahead. Harry tells them they will go about three minutes, stopping five strokes after Mass. Ave. An abbreviated count-down start—"3, 2, 1, attention, go!"—and they fly off. A few strokes in, Harry yells, "Get 'er going, get 'er going!" and then leaves them to it for nearly a thousand meters with no comments. The 3V is dropped very quickly by the others. The freshmen and JV are dead level for nearly the entire piece, with the freshmen taking a couple of seats by the end. The varsity push out to nearly a full length in the first half, then sit on the JV's bow deck, apparently unable to break free. Approaching the bridge, Harry picks up the megaphone again. "Good! Stay on it! Stay strong!"

A few minutes later, the crews have spun and are paddling upstream toward the bridge. The second piece will be three minutes on the clock, starting from the paddle, with ten high strokes before settling to race pace. Harry tells his crews to use this piece to rehearse the second half of the race, to prepare for a strong third five hundred against Northeastern on Saturday. This time he starts the varsity down on the JV, but they take back a total of one length during the piece. The JV take half a length or more from the freshmen, and the 3V manages to hold the frosh for much of the piece and finish only half a length down. As all four crews scream past the MIT boathouse, Harry yells, "Last minute! Push it out! Yeah! Stronger! Stronger!" Twenty strokes later: "Last ten! Stronger!" Approaching the crews as they rest after the piece, he tells them it was "really good." On the weekend, he says, they will need to do the same thing: "Apply relentless pressure."

Thursday, as usual, is a technique and rhythm day, and somehow Harry has arranged for more perfect weather. They do pauses at the finish and out over the toes. "Together on the finishes," says Harry. "Squeeze it in, hands away level." They do the pauses by sixes, and then all eight. Both crews do them with nearly perfect balance when they row all eight. Their bodies are still. Harry looks carefully at the movements immediately after each pause. The varsity five-man needs to move his hands more quickly out over his knees to keep up with the seven-man. The four-man needs to slow down in the second half of the recovery, so the second pause forces him to think about it. When they start rowing continuously, Harry emphasizes control and a "careful approach" as they roll toward the catch. They reach the middle of the Basin, and Harry has them row with a close grip, the outside hand shifted down the handle near the inside hand. "Really feel the draw from the catch all the way through," says Harry. Still with this close grip, they go to three-quarter pressure from Mass. Ave. all the way to the bottom of the Basin. This morning they will row three more lengths of the basin at low cadence, and then do one final stretch from BU up to Weeks. Each time they spin, they begin with twenty strokes at quarter-slide before lengthening out to full strokes, something Harry has been doing with his crews for a couple of years. With such short drive and recovery phases, there is less time to correct for clumsy catches and finishes. They must develop coordination to row the quarter-slide with comfort and balance.

On the way upstream, Harry smells bacon on the air, maybe from a BU dorm. He is telling me about the unfortunate perils of eating bacon when he glances at the JV and interrupts himself, calling out, "That's it, port! Right on the catch together!"

The third of May is overcast and chilly. A stiff east wind blows from the sea, bringing forty-degree air and whipping up choppy water in the Basin. It is the home course for both teams racing for the Smith Cup. The Northeastern men have rowed this river as many times as the Harvard men, and they are always tenacious in this race.

Not knowing if the weather will worsen, the coaches reverse the usual order of racing and run the varsity first. It is a battle, and it reminds Harvard that compared with the faster crews in the league, they have a slow start. Northeastern takes more than half a length in the first five hundred meters before Harvard's grinding base speed tells, and they pull back to within a few seats. But at Massachusetts Avenue someone catches a crab and all the gains are given right back to Northeastern, who again sit six seats up. Harvard must do it all over again, with only a thousand meters to go. They creep, creep, creep, in the increasingly choppy water. With ten strokes to go the crews are level, and Harvard is sprinting for their lives. Their bow slips ahead just before the line. The official margin is 0.7 second.

The JV have a much easier time of it, taking open water before the bridge and hardly even bothering to fight off Northeastern's furious sprint, which gives them a few seats of overlap on the line. Northeastern has no third varsity, so Harvard's 3V and 4V race BU today (BU finishes in between the two). Bill's first boat pulls out to the biggest margin of the day, a full ten seconds over Northeastern. They are undefeated and primed, as in so many previous years, to chase a win at the Eastern Sprints.

Harry, despite the warmth of success, is feeling the chill this morning. In between races, as alumni and parents are jumping in and out of coaching launches at the MIT docks, Harry hops out himself and does some calisthenics, squatting up and down in his rain gear to keep his body warm. Back in his launch Harry gets a phone call from Al Shealy '75, the stroke of the Rude and Smooth crews, who wonders how the day's racing is going. Jim Crick '88, the coxswain for a few years of excellent Harvard crews, watches the races then returns to Newell to chat. He marvels at Harry from across the dock: "He doesn't get older, does he?"

Baden Ireland '02

My junior year was a frustrating one because I was unable to compete as a result of a nagging lower back injury. Leading up to senior year I had come to grips with the fact that my body was telling me it was time to hang up the oar and pursue other things. I still had a strong feeling of dedication and loyalty to HUBC however, so I approached Harry and asked if he could use an assistant coach. He said he could use my help and that opened the door to a tremendous opportunity for me to give back to the program and to experience the sport, as well as get to know Harry from a different perspective.

Fellow teammates were always really interested in little stories about Harry and what would go on in the launch on days when I rode along with him. When I did ride with him, he didn't give me a lot of pointers. He would usually do his thing and make little comments here and there on somebody's catch or perhaps the waterfowl that he had a surprising interest in. There were also long periods of silence that were awkward at first and I would try to break it with random conversation, often unsuccessfully. I learned quickly though when to shoot the shit and when to shut up and let the man do his magic.

Probably the funniest experience riding with Harry was a spring morning in the basin when following the 1V from a distance we suddenly ran out of gas! After unsuccessfully waving the crew down and without a cell phone or a paddle for that matter, we were in the ridiculous situation of floating down river toward Boston. We started actually paddling, Harry with the old megaphone and me with my bare hand, toward the Boston shore across from MIT and got out at a pretty quiet stretch of shoreline. We stood there for a good long while not knowing what to do, with no other crew or boat in sight. Finally a runner came by and we borrowed his cell phone and called Bill at the boathouse. Bill finally arrived with gas can and funnel in hand to save the day and, with few words exchanged, Harry filled the tank and we motored away leaving Bill in our wake in the slower launch.

I was amazed and really thankful for how Harry got me right into things pretty quickly. I had a launch that was pretty much mine that happened to be the newest-looking thing around. In the late spring when I was working mostly with the 3V he gave me a lot of flexibility with lineups and workouts. I remember one of the proudest moments I had was when we were doing basin shots with the three crews and, after the first piece when 3V guys were able to hang in there against a very strong 2V, Harry came by and said "Well, I haven't seen them row better." Coming from Harry it made me feel pretty good.

CHAPTER 8—MAY

Great Day!

IN THE TWO WEEKS REMAINING BEFORE THE EASTERN SPRINTS, THERE are no races against other schools, so there is no need to taper this week. Harry plans to keep pushing them through the weekend. Tuesday morning is two sets of three two-minute pieces with very little rest in between. Before they launch, Harry walks down to the dock and the varsity surround him in a small circle as he talks to them about the workout. They are still and quiet as he speaks. He nods occasionally, and sometimes his right hand comes up and gestures repeatedly, like he's making casts with a tiny fishing rod. When he finishes he claps his hands once as he turns to walk away.

Harry's top two boats and Bill's first boat warm up downstream and line up at the western end of the Basin. Bill is in the launch with Harry, enjoying the opportunity to watch his crew without driving and actively coaching. He may get in a few words periodically, when the launch happens to be near his crew, but mostly he lets Harry run the workout, and leaves the freshmen to get through it as best they can without him. As they follow the crews downstream, Bill tells Harry about his bow-man, who recently confessed he did not want to go to Henley, if his crew wins the Sprints. (The longstanding assumption at Harvard is that if you win the Eastern Sprints, the Friends of Harvard Crew will send you to England.) Clearly the squad had been talking about it, and this rower had not known what Bill's attitude would be. The sense, perhaps, was that if the crew earned the trip, everyone would be expected to sign on enthusiastically, and the bow-man was worried his reticence would be unwelcome. Bill told the young man he needn't worry. The crew could still go without him, and no one would pressure him to go if he didn't want to. "Good for him for bringing it up," says Harry, "rather than letting it fester."

It is a warm and very bright morning in the basin. Four Radcliffe crews are doing basin pieces up ahead. Harry lines up his three crews just upstream from the finish line. They do a brief racing start and then settle quickly, go for two minutes, then paddle for only a few strokes before Harry stops them and lines them up again, checking his watch the whole time to make sure he restarts them after the correct interval. The JV and freshmen are, as on the first piece, almost dead level from start to finish, while the varsity push out to a lead of six seats or so. In the third piece the JV start to gain some ground on the frosh, with the varsity still a little more than half a length up; Harry comments that the varsity guys are "more savvy" about marshalling their energy and anticipating the upcoming work. They make sure to win, but haven't hurt themselves too much yet. As the crews finish this length of the Basin, they almost run out of river—they must stop abruptly and check the boat on the port side to avoid running aground near the Community Sailing boathouse.

The second set is the same format, except two beats higher on all pieces. "Whaddaya say!" says Harry, before they start. By the time they reach the top end of the basin again, after a total of only twenty minutes, each crew will have sprinted the equivalent of two races, always with two crews overlapping them, and with very little rest. It is intense and demanding work. Harry's voice is gravelly, intense and trembling, when he yells through the megaphone: "Keep on them! That's *Brown* over there, that's *Brown* over there! Drive away, drive away, drive away! Keep the pressure on! Be strong!" After the second piece of the second set, Harry tells the JV four-man that his finish is too low, and he needs to hold the blade in and finish more strongly. The four-man replies that his back isn't feeling good, and Harry tells the crew "you'll have to paddle in." As he turns his attention to the other two boats, looking at his watch and getting them lined up, the JV look generally disappointed, and the bow-man scowls. The four-man says, "We want to do the last piece—I can do it," but Harry waves them off and starts the other crews, even as the bow pair of the JV are starting to bring their boat forward to line up.

On the last piece, the varsity take nearly a full-length lead on the freshmen in a matter of twenty strokes. Halfway through, Harry starts yelling through the megaphone, pausing for a few seconds between bursts. "Drive it out! . . . Be stronger! . . . Test yourself! . . . Use it up! . . . Be stronger! . . . Last ten, use it up!" They take their last stroke and immediately stop rowing and collapse over their oars, heaving and grimacing. Harry tells them, "Really well done, well raced." As they finally, weakly, start moving their limbs again, Harry reminds them what this workout is for: "testing yourself, pushing the limits back a little." Bill muses about his crew, who got a very quick brush-off in this last piece: "Well, they're not thinking about Henley now! . . . It's a good lesson for them."

The next day Harry and Bill's crews are training together again, and it is another beautiful day. "Amazing weather," says Harry, following the crews up the stretch above Eliot Bridge. "Three days in a row! It would be a great time to be at Red Top." It will be nearly a month until the team goes to their private training quarters for the Harvard-Yale Race, and in that month they have two major championship regattas to get through. It is too early to yearn for it—the sparkling wide river, the purr of the Seamaster launch, a relaxed early evening, roaming on the grass between the freshmen quarters and the dining hall—but Harry yields for a moment to the memory and anticipation of that unique time and place.

As the crews warm up, Harry and Bill talk recruiting. It is time for admitted students to be pulled off the waiting list, and they talk about which potential rowers to push for, and how many. And then Harry looks up and talks to a rower about his catch: "square *then* drop, keep the blade clear before lifting your hands. Turn the shoulders instead of *reaching* more." Then he is back in the boat, talking with Bill about next year's freshman class.

———

The last week leading up to the Sprints feels easy, but anticipation is building. The rows are easy on Monday and Tuesday, just keeping everyone moving together. On Wednesday Harry's guys start going fast again, but for only twenty strokes at a time, and only building up to rate thirty or thirty-two, not quite reaching race cadence. Thursday and Friday include racing pieces again, enough to feel fast and confident, and nurture that anticipation for the weekend, but not enough to exhaust.

The freshmen are relaxed and joking these days, which Bill likes. He doesn't want them too tense. They join the varsity on Wednesday for three ninety-second pieces, two of them with a racing start, one more like the middle, or "body," of the race. They have rehearsed their full pre-race warmup routine. Bill is happy with his first boat, full of experienced racers from various high school crews, but he worries about the second freshmen: He does not know how they will handle the unknown, and from Bill's perspective, the worst thing is surprise.

Since the racing work takes so little time, Bill focuses on technique for a while, having his crews row with their blades "quarter-feathered" on the recovery, neither square nor flat, but in between, forcing cleaner releases and more controlled blade heights. The three-man in Bill's first boat pipes up and says he prefers a full feather, because it is easier. "Bad answer," says Bill. That is exactly why they are doing the drill! Bill tells the coxswain that the crew can row with the normal, full feather, until the three-man's blade looks different than the other starboard blades, and then switch to quarter-feather. He holds out for fifteen minutes.

Bill has to bring together freshmen who have rowed for lots of different coaches at their various schools, and convince them, now, to listen to his instruction. He likes it when they say, "Why don't we do it this way, that's how we did it at school?" Bill's response: "Well, this year we have to be better than your high school." Aha.

The middle of May is nesting time for the flock of geese who occupy the scrub and the rocks just upstream from the BU Bridge. Harry eyes a nest accusingly, and reports that he has, at some indeterminate time in the past, put oil on the eggs to keep them from hatching. This is the "approved method," he says. (Will a new line appear on the tally board in the shop, an image of a nest of eggs to go along with the geese, squirrels, rats, and mice?)

Harry cannot afford to let up on the technical coaching either. The "uptight" varsity three-seat is told to hold onto the pressure at the finish, by pushing his legs, and also to extend himself and reach out his hands as he comes up the slide: "Don't wrap your hand around the oar, keep the wrist flat." Can the varsity beat Brown? "That's the plan," says Harry, but it will take a good race. This is not a year of domination, so every bit of precision, every ounce of focus, will count. The group of coaches who produce the final seedings for the Sprints have ranked Harvard third, behind Brown and Wisconsin and ahead of Princeton and Northeastern. To be sure, they had a horrible dual race against Brown in the Stein Cup, on that rough-water day at the beginning of the season. But Harry is more sobered by the series of margins that Brown has put down against other crews in the league: They have beaten both Princeton and Northeastern by over a length, whereas Harvard squeaked out those wins by a second at most.

The championship regatta of the Eastern Association of Rowing Colleges takes place all in one day in Worcester, Massachusetts. Morning heats may qualify a crew for one of the afternoon finals (Grand or Petite). In the previous dozen years, Harvard's varsity, JV, and freshman crews have on average placed third at the Eastern Sprints. The league consists of the entire Ivy League plus several other universities: Boston University, Northeastern, MIT, the Naval Academy, Rutgers, Syracuse, the University of Wisconsin (who are closer to Massachusetts than to California, where the western league has traditionally raced), and more recently Georgetown and Holy Cross. Since Bill Manning began coaching the freshmen, they have done no worse than fourth place, and that was once, eight years ago. The varsity average is closer to silver than bronze during the previous decade. To qualify for the Grand Final of six crews, they must place first or second in their morning race. They have done this every year since 1964.

For two years in a row, 1969 and 1970, Penn beat Harvard in the Adams Cup, and in both years Harvard returned the favor by beating out Penn to win the Grand Final of the Eastern Sprints. In the 1970 race the two crews were dead level for fifteen hundred meters, and then Harvard pulled away to win by half a length. Harry described the race as "perfect, just perfect," and called it "the most satisfying victory of my career," just as he had the year before. These were the last two years that Penn was coached by Joe Burk.

The pre-regatta seedings determine which crews will face each other in the morning heats. Crews are placed into the heats by setting out a chart—three rows of six spots each, representing three qualifying heats—and then laying down the numbers 1 through 18 in boustrophedon: first top to bottom (1, 2, 3) and then bottom to top (4, 5, 6), and then top to bottom again (7, 8, 9), until the chart is full. Thus the heats are: (1, 6, 7, 12, 13, 18), (2, 5, 8, 11, 14, 17), and (3, 4, 9, 10, 15, 16). How hard it is to reach the Grand Final, by finishing first or second in your heat, depends on where the speed is clustered in the field. The difference between the 7th and 12th seed may sound big, but it may be less than a length, well within the margin of racing strategy, momentum, and inspiration.

Throughout the morning, the Harvard's heavyweight crews perform as expected. Most of them are seeded first in their races, and they justify that by winning their heats: First Freshmen, Second Varsity, Third Varsity (followed closely by the Fourth Varsity, rowing in the same event and finishing second in the same heat). And then, just before lunch, the Varsity Heavyweights come down the lake.

In the first two heats, the top two seeds qualify for the Grand Final: Brown and Columbia, Wisconsin and Northeastern. In the third heat, Harvard faces #4 Princeton, #9 Cornell, and #10 Yale. Harry suspects that Yale is faster than Cornell. This is the first time Harvard and Yale have seen each other this season, and there is always motivation to beat them. Harvard and Yale are the historically essential rivalry in this sport in America, at least on the East Coast. And while Harry has been involved, the balance has been firmly in Harvard's favor.

In the opening quarter of the race, Harvard is down to Princeton and Yale. This is a familiar scenario, though—they rely on their ability to wear down their opponents with a steady, relentless middle thousand and, when necessary, a powerful final sprint. It is what everyone expects from Harvard crews. And for a while the typical race seems to be working as they claw back, slowly, into Yale. But Princeton remains stubbornly a few seats ahead, and Harvard decides to sprint early, taking up the rating not long into the last five hundred meters. They move ahead of Yale, but not for long. It is a gamble to try breaking Yale's confidence so far from the finish, and it does not work. Yale uses their own sprint to squeeze back through, as Harvard tries to hold on. Princeton, Yale, and Harvard finish in that order with less than a second separating them, leaving a full length of clear water, more than six seconds, back to Cornell. The finish is close enough that the crews sit in their shells, near the bridge by the finish line, waiting for the official results and the realization that Harvard will not race in the Grand Final.

Sportswriters "are always looking at streaks," Harry reflects some weeks later. "But it's basically meaningless. It's not an issue. We knew going into it that the heats were going to be tough, the crews would be very even with one another, we'd gotten a sort of unlucky draw. We lost by a very narrow margin to two very good crews. That's it." It is always disappointing to miss a marker like qualification for a final. Losing to Yale in particular is needling, and especially since Yale won last year's Harvard-Yale Race in a fashion that was glorious for them and devastating for Harvard. The weight of forty-four consecutive Grand Finals has no effect on Harry Parker? "No, not in the least." But for the rest of that day, Harry is subdued. He is pensive, but not angry. His crew raced courageously, they pushed themselves to their limit. There is nothing wrong with being sixth best in the world, Harry told his 1968 Olympians. His varsity's best case scenario for this year's Sprints is seventh.

In the first final of the afternoon, the Second Freshmen win their final-only event. Not long after, the Third and Fourth Varsity eights finish ahead of all other third boats, and the First Freshmen fend off Princeton and Brown to win by a second, earning a trip to Henley if they want it. The JV fight wire-to-wire against last year's winners, Wisconsin, who take the Sprints title again by two-tenths of a second. This is the first race all season that the JV have lost. The varsity end their day with a second-place finish in the Petite Final, outraced by the Naval Academy. Underperformance, compared with the rest of the squad, is unusual for Harry's top boat. The complete, outright success of the freshmen mixes oddly with the disappointment in the higher varsity boats. It is time for the squad to reflect and regroup, and it is time for Harry to tinker.

Justin Bosley '03

One spring afternoon in 2002, the varsity was trying out a new eight, manufactured by King. Apparently, King finally felt that the necessary composite materials were available to build an eight in his traditional design. Harvard had obtained one of the early prototypes and we were trying it out. We didn't, however, well, like it. At all. The hull didn't accelerate through the stroke and gave the sensation of a stiff drive and sluggish recovery. Harry insisted we try it though, and we used it for some racing pieces in the Powerhouse Stretch. The JV destroyed the varsity that day. There was no dynamic rowing, no power, no responsiveness within the shell. After the row, Harry pulled the varsity aside and basically told us we were not trying hard enough. I think it was the first time I witnessed Harry searching for words to adequately express his thoughts. Or perhaps he was just trying to remain professional and diplomatic. Typically, Harry's thoughts are clear and straightforward, and he can find words to convey them as such. In this irritated and pissed off state though, he would hesitate, searching for words. He often shakes his head when giving instruction or correcting someone, and his head was shaking nearly throughout the conversation. His right hand was making its traditional chopping motion too, emphasizing his points. He agreed that the equipment didn't suit us, but he was disappointed that we didn't seem to give it a fair try.

The weeks between the Sprints and the national championship regatta, held under the auspices of the Intercollegiate Rowing Association, are a time of broken routines. Classes are over, and the rowers must fit their training around study sessions and then final exams. They train indoors on their own, they find partners and row in pairs, and Harry gets the crews together as much as he can. He mixes up the varsity and JV rowers to make two even crews, reminiscent of February and March, and they spend a couple of days side-by-side, with some seat-racing between the eights. The second boat has been so consistently fast, so impressive in their races, that he tries to locate and tap the best of that ability and transpose it into the varsity. It does not work. In the end, the same men remain in the two boats, but the varsity's seating arrangement is altered. Perhaps the different flow of communication, of both words and rhythm, will make for a livelier, more efficient, more racy crew.

Meanwhile, since there is no Third Varsity eight at the IRA regatta, Wayne Berger takes the best from those two crews and manages to enter them as a second JV entry. It is rare to see this, but this Harvard squad has unusual depth.

For years, at this time in the year, Harvard would wait for Commencement and then decamp to Gales Ferry, Connecticut, spending as much as two weeks at their private training quarters preparing to race Yale. The IRA regatta went on for a century without these two, who would not sacrifice the tradition of the one for the wider perceived importance of the other. The rest of the top flight of American collegiate rowing gathered for four days without them. Sometimes Harvard or Yale might contend for the only official National Championship, a smaller invitation-only regatta in Cincinnati later in June, but some of Harvard's "unofficial" national titles were because they beat Washington separately, when Washington had beaten everyone else together. When finally they joined the crowd in the mid-1990s, it was a shock to see, all of a sudden, the sea of crimson shirts that had been absent for so long.

Harry raced for the University of Pennsylvania in the old days of the IRA, when the regatta had recently relocated from Poughkeepsie to Syracuse and was a much simpler affair. Lake Onondaga (like the Hudson for so many previous years) was wide enough that there was no need for the Olympic-style progression of six-lane heats, repechages, semifinals, and finals. All fifteen crews simply lined up side by side, and when the cannon went off, they all raced for the finish line three miles away. Cornell was the powerhouse in the mid-1950s, and even Harry's Henley-winning 1955 crew lost to them at the IRA. In 1956, though, Penn trained for some days in Ithaca before a dual race with Cornell over two-and-a-third miles. Harry recalls a "brutal" race with crews overlapping the whole way down the course. He was part of the bow four, who thought of themselves as a unit and had their own special contribution to the race plan, a forty-stroke sprint that was supposed to come a quarter-mile from the finish. But this time, "the four-man called it at a half-mile to go, instead of a quarter-mile to go, so we just went flat-out for forty strokes, and then found out we had forty more strokes, and we were done . . . And we won it by a third of a length, or a deck-length or something like that, and we were just totally exhausted. We could hardly row back to the boathouse." A week later, with a rower being substituted due to injury, Cornell won the IRA, but that hard-fought victory remains one of Harry's favorite racing memories.

As the coach buses take Harvard south to begin their final series of races, the top end of Harry's squad roll toward New Jersey with a lot hanging over their heads. The JV want to avenge their only loss of the year, but the varsity's need for redemption is deeper, more fraught, and keener. Not only were they left out of the final, finishing lower at the Sprints than Harvard should ever do, but it was Yale, of all teams, who knocked them out.

When the heats for the varsity eight are posted, Harvard finds that they share the first heat with Brown and Yale. Redemption is available from their first race. There are some practicalities on the line in addition to their pride. A top-two finish in the heat will qualify them for the semis two days later. Not only would this mean a day without racing, as the rest of the semis are determined in the "repechage" races, but the seniors have arranged to return to Harvard for graduation ceremonies on that very day. If they do not qualify from the first race, they will have to stay in New Jersey. Keeping all this in mind, they open this regatta with an attack. They chase Brown, the Eastern Sprints champions, all the way down the course, holding them to half a length. Yale has no answer for this speed, and finish open-water down on Harvard. So far, so good.

The JV finish second in their heat too, the third boat is third in theirs, and the freshmen win. Then, over the next three days, amid schedule changes due to weather, the various Harvard heavyweight crews shuttle back and forth to the hotel, eat, read, nap, have short paddles up and down the course, and generally take alternate between either relaxing and letting the nerves out, or priming themselves for six-minute bursts of intensity and furious action. (The seniors do indeed fly back to Cambridge for graduation exercises.) Harry shepherds the crews and has quiet talks with them by the trailer, in their rooms, or in the shade of the trees alongside the Cooper River. They hear the usual words: be persistent, grind them down. Harry's hand rises and falls, his feet shuffle, his voice is sometimes so soft that the guys have to lean in to hear him. Trust yourself that you can keep going. Stay strong.

This IRA regatta is not one of Harvard's best. The freshmen, having won their heat, return to win their semifinal as well. But California and Washington appear together in the other semifinal race, where they finish very strongly in that order. They do it again on finals day, leaving Harvard behind by open water to finish third, just half a length ahead of Yale. The JV earn their spot in the Grand Final by finishing third in their semi, and then manage a distant fourth place in that final, behind Washington, California, and Wisconsin. It is a good performance for this crew, and entirely consistent with their results this spring, but it does not match their hopes. The bow-man thinks they thought too much of themselves after winning in San Diego, and kept that "golden crew" attitude through the season. They never regained their rhythm after the turmoil following the Sprints.

In some ways the varsity eight's semifinal tells the story of their season. They finish in a disappointing fifth place, which puts them once again in the Petite Final rather than the Grands. Demonstrating their dominance of the heavyweight field this year, Washington and California take the first two spots in this semi, within a second of each other and a full length up on Northeastern, who are in turn a length ahead of Navy. Both of these eastern crews lost to Harvard in the regular season before placing ahead of them at the Sprints, and to be sure there is some history and grudging here. But the more crucial result in this race was against Yale, who race alongside all the way down the course and finish within two-tenths of a second behind.

On finals day, when Wisconsin has the sprint of the season and takes down Washington and Cal for the national title, the varsity do little more than limp down the course to place fifth in the Petites, and this time Yale storms ahead of them by three seconds. It is a hard thing to summon a third supreme effort in close succession at the end of a season, when the result does not feel like it matters. Racing for a medal, as the freshmen did, would be one thing, but racing for seventh place is hardly the same. They have made their point against Yale in two races this week: Do they need to do it a third time in four days? And something else, something that matters much more, is so close, only a bus-ride away. Red Top.

Clint Allen '67

I was a football player who came to Harvard with a full scholarship, from a tough neighborhood, as a 220-pound fullback with an all-state, High School All-America resume. Unfortunately I sustained a serious knee injury freshman year and was unable to get a contact eligibility. So I wandered down to the boathouse to see if maybe that was a sport I might like and could do. I met Harry. He seemed nice enough if a little dry. But with few athletic options, I gave it a try. Harry was already a world class rowing coach even as a young man, but from the beginning Harry and I never got on the same page. No two people could have been less simpatico!

A cocky kid, I, of course, liked the stroke seat and spent my sophomore year stroking the third boat, to an undefeated season. I never like practicing, and really never felt the "rush" some oarsman say they got with a perfectly set up, fast boat. But I loved to race and win. I LOVED to compete and I never lost a race in a Harvard boat. Never had to surrender my shirt to a competitor, never lost a seat race and never drank the "Parker Kool Aid" to become a dedicated, totally focused, committed Harry follower.

As much as I'm sure Harry tried, he couldn't keep me out of the first boat my junior year. I simply didn't, wouldn't lose a seat-race and my boats always won. So, there he had it, as *Globe* writer John Ahern described me, "the tough kid from Brockton" sitting in the prestigious Harvard varsity stroke seat. Far from the straight-laced, typical dedicated gentleman oarsman Harry loved, sat a brash kid with no "Groton pedigree" who believed and preached that "there's no such thing as a good loser." And we didn't. I remember the Compton Cup that we won handily; I wore a pair of sunglasses . . . NOBODY had ever done that before and Harry got unhinged! Taking me aside, he chastised me for this great offense. Frankly all I cared about was the win and the glasses kept the sun out of my eyes. And I heard he really got bent out of shape when he saw my Massachusetts license plate STROKE on the back of my Sunbeam Alpine sports car, bought with earnings from my folk singing gigs around town. And so my year ended with a seven-length win over Yale in upstream record time. OK for a walk-on!

The following year, after far too many cortisone shots in my knee before races, my rowing career ended. And I'm guessing with a sigh of relief from Harry. Sure, in those days I was sometimes a "showboat," but I found that the little bit of craziness I took on and off the water worked for me while definitely keeping me from being one of "Harry's favorites." C'est la guerre.

The 2004 edition of the "God Squad," undefeated national champions.
SPORT GRAPHICS

Launching to race at the Head of the Charles, 2010. DAVID PARKER

Talking with the varsity on the dock.

The Red Top boathouse.

With Kathy and Abigail, following a crew home to Red Top.

Following the Yale Race.

After sweeping Yale, before going into the Thames.

After being thrown into the river.

The Rock. ROW2K.COM

Harvard about to nip Leander by a few feet just moments before the finish, Henley Royal Regatta 2012. ROW2K.COM

Harry's last crew, 2013 Eastern Sprints champions. ROW2K.COM

Harry coaches the 1980 Olympic reunion crew, June 2013. SUSAN R. WOOD

Newell Boathouse on the morning of Harry's memorial service. IGOR BELAKOVSKIY

Well Rowed Harvard, Well Rowed Yale (Or, "You're Gonna Love Red Top!")

ONE SPRING MORNING HARRY IS RACING THREE CREWS ALL THE WAY UP the Basin toward BU. The coxswains are pointed straight at the markers on the Boston shore that indicate the racing lanes, but they keep going past the finish line. As they near the BU boathouse and the river gets narrower, Harry tells them "twenty more" but then quickly corrects it to "five more!" when he sees two crews coming downstream out of the bridge. He chuckles that they almost covered the full mile-and-three-quarters racecourse. Until the late 1960s that was the length of races on the Charles, because that was the longest straight distance available for side-by-side racing. Crews nearly ran up onto the Boston shore at the finish. Other courses on other rivers or lakes were set the same way: two miles, two-and-a-third, one-and-five-sixteenths, whatever would fit. Each weekend's race was a different distance than the last. To prepare, crews did time-trials of the appropriate distance during the week, usually on Wednesdays, says Harry. Meanwhile, the Olympic distance was 2,000 meters, a mile-and-a-quarter, and in the 1960s the decision was made to standardize the college races to the Olympic length, in the hope of better training the top rowers for international competition. ("Not that it helped," Harry adds.)

The one match that escaped standardization was the Harvard-Yale Race in New London, which remained a four-miler. It endured other tribulations, however. In the 1970s Yale changed its academic calendar and refused the normal time and setting for The Race. One year it was raced in Boston over three miles, from the bottom of the Basin upstream to the Weeks bridge. In 1974 Harvard traveled across the country to beat West Coast champions Washington over four miles, and along the way beat Wisconsin, the IRA winners, in Milwaukee. The next year Washington came east, and they raced over the Race course in New London. (These were two of the six years Harvard were "unofficially" national champions under Harry, in addition to the ten times they won a recognized national regatta.) Then Harvard raced Navy in New London, too, and soon Yale agreed to a new schedule for The Race. Typically it follows the IRA, and closes the year for the students who take part.

Understatement of the season: It is not just another race. It is, after all, capitalized. The cover of the regatta program reminds the reader that this is "America's Oldest Intercollegiate Athletic Event." It is not the sole reason for the existence of the rowing programs at Harvard and Yale, but it is no small matter that the two squads finish their years with this match, and that each maintains a private facility to house them as they get ready. Their other classic rivalry also goes by a single, capitalized name ("The Game"), and each event's character matches its home venue: the Harvard Stadium is big, glorious, brash. Newell and Red Top are remote (even obscure), quirky, austere. Statistics might show more people associate Harvard vs. Yale with football, rather than rowing, but by historical precedent (twenty-three years) and sheer association with New England tradition, the rowing rivalry trumps. Rowing events around the world, in an attempt to appropriate legitimacy and attract attention, invite famous crews to attend. They pick Oxford, Cambridge, Harvard, and Yale.

For this week in Gales Ferry, the daily life of the Harvard oarsman is redefined. He may not know that this little hamlet in the town of Ledyard has that name, for in the Harvard camp it is always called "Red Top." (The actual namesake top is just the little red roof on the cupola, maybe five feet square, that pokes up from the middle of the boathouse.) If he has not been before, he will have anticipated it, having read descriptions in books and articles, or picked up hints of the traditions passed on by the upperclassmen. Strictly speaking the official residents would be the top two varsity crews, the first freshmen crew, and another eight composed of the best remaining Harvard heavyweights, known as the "Combination" crew. A spare four is often invited to join, and perhaps a couple more at Harry's discretion. For several years the repeated refrain all spring has been, "You're gonna love Red Top."

Things to love:

> The food (catered, ironically, by the Yale dining services, and apparently controlled to the finest detail by Harry);
>
> The grounds, which sprawl across a quarter mile and include grassy lawn, pleasantly erupting rocks, a path through the woods, and five buildings;
>
> Time to relax, with no other burdens;
>
> The train track with the little "Red Top" whistle-stop indicator;
>
> Ping-Pong;
>
> Nightly skits by the freshmen;
>
> Croquet;
>
> Watching for submarines at the Navy base down river;
>
> The beef broth served on the dock after the afternoon row;
>
> The naked plunge into the Thames, preceding or following the beef broth;
>
> Weighing in on the old scale twice a day, and seeing the record of years and years prior, slowly coming undone on the paper still tacked to the wall;
>
> The inscriptions on the doors of the cupboards in the dorms, telling who slept there before and the result of their Race;
>
> If you are a rower, being waited on every meal by the coxswains;
>
> The view of the Rock from the dining hall porch, the Freshmen Quarters, the varsity quarters, or the boathouse.

Things not to love:

If you are a coxswain, waiting on the rowers all week;

The old, nonfunctional plumbing;

Being approached by armed patrol boats near the Navy base;

The nightly skits by the freshmen;

Putting in and taking out the enormous Seamaster launches and the heavy sections of floating dock;

Encountering the wake from a passing Seamaster launch;

The lack of good Internet access.

The nerve center is the dining hall, roughly in the middle of the compound. Two long rows of tables and chairs dominate the open hall, and a small room adjoins on the river side for eating or for board games. The kitchen is at one end, a TV and game room at the other end. Within sight to the north is the Freshmen Quarters, and a few minutes' walk beyond, over a wooden bridge, is the varsity dormitory. The rowers have single rooms, opening onto long shared porches facing the river. They are small and spartan: a bed, a chair, a desk, a small closet. A long hallway runs the length of each floor of the Quarters. The wooden stairs creak.

The Coach's Cabin hides between trees, near the dining hall and almost on the road. It is essentially two rooms and a porch. Harry stays there with Kathy and Abigail. His bike leans against the wall, his golf bag stands next to a tree, his bike shorts hang from the clothesline on the porch.

Harry herds the oarsmen, coaches, and boatman as necessary. He determines practice times and may or may not inform everyone the night before. In the morning he walks the three minutes to the Varsity Quarters and wakes everyone with a knock and perhaps a whistle ("some sort of jazz tune," according to one rower). He typically sits at one end of the table with his family at meal times, and usually stays after dinner for the skits; he waits for a signal to send his daughter away, when the material becomes more mature. Other than the two practices and the meals, the rowers are left alone. They leave the grounds if they wish, even in the evening. Everyone has time to themselves.

On this week several years ago, Harry told a visiting reporter that "when I stop coaching, I'll probably miss this most of all."

—◆—

Kathy Keeler was just inducted into Wesleyan University's new athletic Hall of Fame. Of all Wesleyan alums, Kathy is the only one with an Olympic gold medal. Looking at the roster for the Wesleyan induction ceremony, Kathy was tickled to learn that she would share the stage with New England Patriots coach Bill Belichick and marathon runner Bill Rodgers. Kathy was on four national teams, and coached several others as well as Smith College. She won her Olympic medal as stroke of the US women's eight in 1984, the second time such a crew had raced. The very first Olympic women's eight in 1976 won a bronze, coached by Harry Parker. Kathy qualified for the 1980 team that did not compete due to the boycott, and she met Harry that year in training. They were married five years later, and their daughter Abigail was born five years after that.

Harry's mother, and her circle of friends, would not have been rowers. Harry grew up in a world where women and girls were not expected to do "muscular" activities the way men and boys did. One day this spring, watching a high school girls' four pass his launch on their way back to the Winsor School boathouse, Harry is reflective. "This sounds like a sexist thing to say, or even to think, but I found myself wondering recently, 'why do women row?'" Watching women and girls row, he does not get the sense of bodily power behind the oar handle that is so familiar from the heavyweight men he sees every day. He doesn't see their muscles the same way. "I know that when I row, it's the muscular exertion and the satisfaction that comes from it." Do women experience it the same way he does, he wonders, and thus do it for the same reason? He concludes that they must—it must be the same.

This is the man who coached the very first women's national team from the United States, who married an Olympic gold medalist, whose daughter will soon begin rowing for Winsor School. The women he coached in 1975 and 1976, says Harry, were strong and extraordinary. He did not need to ask himself the question of why they pursued rowing. He was able to see them, and thus treat them, much as he would his male athletes. He pushed them and they responded. He worked to blend their diverse rowing styles and their distinct personalities, and he figured out how to make their boat go very fast. Harry, of all people, could appreciate their persistence. Photographs of the 1976 "Red Rose Crew" look very much like photographs of Harvard crews: faces determined, bodies powerful, legs and torsos not quite lining up.

(Not that it was all straightforward for Harry with these women. He was uncertain and uneasy about the differences between male and female physiology. Did menstrual cycles affect their ability to train? Could they handle the same workload as the men? Until 1988, women's crews raced only 1,000 meters, half the men's distance, with dubious justification. Harry also made an unusual breach of decorum by pursuing romantic involvement with his female athletes.)

As the aloof leader of the most traditional sport at the most elite college, Harry has promoted access. When questions arose about equal support and allocation of resources for the women's team (still known, uniquely, as "Radcliffe"), coach Liz O'Leary says Harry was on board. On a university athletic committee, Harry was the voice of reason, making suggestions that made sense, not necessarily benefiting himself and his program. ("He's the voice you want whispering in your ear.")

As a fellow coach, says O'Leary, Harry has been "a wonderful blend of supportive when I asked for help and quiet when I didn't." He watches the Radcliffe crews, but he does it subtly. He once watched her varsity race from a car on Memorial Drive, surprising her later by saying "Well done, that's a fast crew you have there." The ultimate compliment from Harry, says O'Leary, is "well done." She hangs out in the shop at Newell sometimes, hoping to get Harry to say something. She asks him what he has figured out about rigging, or the new oar designs. When she has asked for help, he has never said no. "I feel like I have an advantage over every other women's rowing coach in the country. No one else has a Harry Parker."

As the assumed leader and guru of all things related to rowing in Boston, Harry wielded the influence to expand community access to rowing. When plans were developed to build a new boathouse above the North Beacon Street bridge to replace the shoestring facilities used by several schools, colleges, and Community Rowing, Incorporated, Harry talked to his friends and encouraged them to support it. The result, a remarkable and exciting new presence on the river, was named in Harry's honor. CRI's motto is "rowing for all."

Kathy Keeler, though not part of the team, is part of the family. She, Abigail, and the Parkers' dog Pika, appear in various combinations at Newell throughout the year, in the lounge, on the dock, in the coaching launch. Kathy will walk right into a boat meeting—something other rowers on the squad would never do—and contribute a comment. The Harvard rowing family and the Parker family are separated by a permeable line, and there is some room for debate about who draws it and where it lies. It has always been thus: Before the final race of the 1968 Olympic Trials, Harry read the crew a letter from seven-year-old George, challenging the crew to miniature golf.

Here at Red Top it all comes together for Harry: the family, the boathouse family, the extended Harvard rowing family, the rowing family. Though it seems closed, separate, exclusive, the atmosphere here is more familial than an outsider might expect. Physically the property is open, with large green lawns separating buildings, big porches, screen doors, open space everywhere, no fences or barriers. Newell Boathouse feels far more private than this. Red Top welcomes you. Yale alumni join Harvard alumni on Race day for a luncheon under a big tent on the bluff above the boathouse. They are welcome. Sometimes other coaches have slept in the little attic room of the Coach's Cabin. There is no privacy in the cabin. Harry is happy to offer the space to someone who needs it.

As a young girl Abigail would play with the boys, usually drawn to one or two "favorites" for conversations and fun. At Red Top she and the caretaker's daughter would draw pictures and compose poems, to be presented to the team at dinnertime. A story floated that when she was asked at school what word started with "Y," she replied, "the enemy." As a teenager she is less involved with the team (the Internet is available via dial-up in the cabin), but she is no stranger. She joins Harry and Kathy in the launch to watch practice, and afterward the boys attempt some discretion when they slip off their towels and slip naked into the river.

The received opinion is that Harry's personality has changed recently, that he has "softened." Harry claims to have no idea what this is about. He is just as competitive as he ever was, he says, just as determined to win whenever and however possible. Recent results bear this out. And he is still a man to be avoided when impatient or frustrated, a man you are afraid of disappointing. But recent generations of Harvard rowers and observers have seen something real enough to give it a name: the Abigail Factor. Scott McMullin '96 recalls that Harry's "best emotion and expression was the big smile and laugh he had when he was happy, like when crews were winning or when he was with Abigail." Does having a young daughter change his interactions with the young men he leads? After nearly fifty years, Harry surely has relaxed into his rhythm, increased the ratio of banter to exhortation. Though the oarsmen of the 2000s still tread lightly around Harry, and still make comparisons to the Deity, they would not now feel the need to nickname him "the Old PF" (a bitter combination of two common curse words). And one doubts that the men of the 1970s would have witnessed Harry scurrying along the side of the Old Tanks, chasing a small dog and calling "Here, Pika-Pika. . . ."

Arriving in Gales Ferry this year, everyone is excited for The Race, which is a week away. A week to soak up Red Top, to recover from the stress and disappointment of the IRA, to redefine themselves as Harvard crews participating in their own family event, a milestone and marker of their identity, of their particular tribe. Other schools have ivy, but they do not have this.

It is hot on the Thames for the first couple of days, and the river is totally exposed to the sun. They settle into the daily routines of weighing in, showering, eating, napping. On the river, they become familiar with the racecourse: New London's Gold Star Bridge, where most varsity races start, the Coast Guard Academy, the sub-base, Buoy 13, Red Top, the Rock. On Monday they row twice, down the course and back, but do no hard work. Tuesday the effort ramps up to a couple of one- and two-mile pieces, and then on Wednesday three twelve-minute building pieces that end at full pressure, the varsity and JV chasing down the freshmen. The weather is clear, the crews feel lively, and good spirits reign. In between the oarsmen seek out wi-fi at Dunkin' Donuts out on Route 12. They sleep, play video games, practice cards to prepare for a casino visit. They lament the "rustic" conditions in the Quarters.

Since The Race is four miles, and they have been so focused on the two-kilometer distance all spring, Harry usually stages a "time trial" during the Red Top camp, reminiscent of the old days when each week the race distance would change. The time itself is not the crucial part, but rather the rehearsal of a race at this distance, the mental preparation for a sustained effort of that length. All four crews participate, but only the varsity is a four-miler. The JV will race three miles, the freshmen and Combination crew only two. For the time trial, the Combis start level with the varsity and race the first two miles only. One mile upriver, the JV are waiting. They sit ready, and when the bow of the varsity reaches their stern, a coach says "go!" and they begin their three-mile race to the finish line. A racing start from a dead stop puts them at full racing speed just as the other crew comes level. (An assistant coach is in charge of this tricky start, and if it is not done correctly Harry will snap at him.) One mile later, the freshmen do the same, starting just at the moment the Combis finish, and now once again there are three crews racing to the end. By the time the freshmen start their race, the varsity have already been racing side-by-side for nine minutes, and now a totally fresh crew appears to test them for another nine. In the face of this, the varsity typically outlast the frosh and cross the line first. Now they know what it means to really race for four miles.

All year Harry has kept The Race in his mind. Every once in a while the crews have battled for four miles up or down the Charles, usually head-style (chasing each other, not side-by-side), with the familiar building profile to keep them on their toes and pushing right to the end. Whether or not they knew it, Harry was keeping their bodies primed for the long haul. The Race is a full mile longer than the head races they experienced last fall, and there are no bends, no parade of other crews to work through or push off of. Just a straight open course with one opponent to outwit or outlast or otherwise defeat. At Red Top Harry may decide the best crew for the four-miler is not the same as it was for the two-thousand-meter sprint season. He may change the stroke, or swap men between the varsity and JV. The energy and interactions in the crew may need to be adjusted for this race.

And Harry knows that the rhythm of life at Red Top, the separation from the familiar routines, may pull the athletes off their best. A few years ago, when Yale was relatively weak, he reprimanded a crew who had dominated their spring season, for not winning a practice piece convincingly enough one day. "I don't mean to suggest that anyone was consciously holding back, but unconsciously I think it was happening. Maybe because you're not expecting Yale to offer the same kind of challenge you have had up to now. It's so easy for it to happen, to work not at 100 percent but just short of it."

The four-miler is different, and upsets happen. Though Harry has lost this race exactly seven times since 1963, the last two were upsets, including last year. In 2007 Harvard and Yale were gold and silver at the Sprints with two seconds between them, and Yale was only one second slower in the same semifinal race at the IRA. In The Race Harvard took half a length almost immediately, pulled away steadily, and held an open-water lead for the duration, but Yale did not give in. After the last half-mile flag they pushed, and Harvard could not hold on. The verdict was half a second to Yale. Harvard's five-man was taken to the hospital and treated for exhaustion. "Incredible, just incredible," said Harry. Nothing like this had happened in years, if ever. When Yale walked through Harvard to win in 1999 it happened much earlier, and the final result was much more convincing. Fewer than ten Races have finished with margins under five seconds. Close margins come in pairs: 1937–38, 1948–49, 1994–95. Harry does not want to be on the losing side of a close one again.

Harry's first ever varsity win in The Race was, of course, an upset. Five years ago the new varsity shell, as usual a pale yellow Empacher, was dedicated in the name of Geoffrey Picard '65, who stroked the varsity for three years, beginning with that dramatic win in 1963. He was part of the heartbreaking Olympic effort in 1964, and then the 1965 crew started breaking course records wherever they went. One newspaper report led to another, *Time* and *Newsweek* chimed in, and then *Sports Illustrated* put them on the cover, "which some people thought was a good thing," remarked Harry.

But at the christening ceremony on the dock, on Race day fifty years later, Harry said that his fondest memories of Picard were from that first year, at Red Top. The crew had not made the Grand Final of the Eastern Sprints. On the Thames, after some failed attempts to jump-start the crew with high-rate work, Harry reversed course and took them down, redefining their rhythm at a low stroke rate.

Race day was very windy, "but not so bad we couldn't send out the freshmen." They won, but referees decided to postpone the longer races until the following morning. The sixteenth of June dawned "absolutely gorgeous," and for the first time ever, the huge bare rock across the river had been painted with a huge red H. "We just knew it would be a great day," said Harry—and here he paused, choking up and wiping his eyes—"and it was."

The Race was downstream that year. Harvard were trailing Yale as they passed the Rock during the opening strokes of the race, but with their new rhythm and new confidence and the persistence that they would bequeath to fifty more years of Harry's crews, they worked their way back through Yale and won by more than seven boat-lengths. A great day.

While other crewmates of Geoff Picard shared their memories, Harry ducked back into the boathouse to dab his eyes. He reemerged to hug Picard's widow warmly and then pour champagne for everyone. There, with his former oarsmen, Harry was shining, a social and vibrant version of himself that the current team rarely sees. One of the freshmen told me he had just heard Harry speak more than he had all year.

On Wednesday afternoon Harry takes out the varsity and JV for a series of drills and twenty- and thirty-stroke bursts. They row with only their outside arm, each watching his blade as it glides and hovers a few inches above the water's surface before dropping out of sight again. They sit in calm water and practice the recovery sequence, rolling the seat, controlling the handle, placing the blade in the water. Harry tells the captain to "stay steady at the front end," that he wants the wheels still rolling as he puts the blade in. They do their twenties and thirties at just below race cadence, focusing on application of power, adding speed during the last ten of each set. He points out to the crews the contrast between the headwind and the tailwind, the need to deliberately push the hands out into the headwind to maintain their rhythm. Back in the boathouse after the row, Harry gestures across to the Rock, a blue blotch with a giant white "Y" in the middle. Look at it, he says. Keep it in mind these last few days.

After breakfast Harry heads off campus for coffee and a newspaper (the dining hall does not serve coffee, though sometimes they will brew some special in the kitchen). He wanders around the dining hall, talking with Joe, closing windows in the small side nook. The press are coming today, and this is where they will eat. Joe wants to put a tablecloth out, but Harry jokes, "What, you want to make them feel welcome?" Yale is keeping the press off their property this year, holding their press meeting in a park.

Harry spends an hour before lunch in the shade behind the Coach's Cabin, practicing his golf swing. In the past he might have participated in the team croquet tournament, reportedly cheating ruthlessly. Now he is more likely to head off for a round of golf or a bike ride. When Dave Wagener '76 showed up a few years ago with his own bike, Harry offered one-, two-, or three-hour routes, and lobbied for the longer option. Kathy, on the other hand, does not bike with Harry. "He's *good!*" she says. She had hoped, since he is several years her senior, that as they aged he would eventually slow down more quickly than she did—and here she draws curves in the air which eventually intersect—but it has not happened yet.

Later that morning, chairs are arranged in a small oval on the cement porch on the west side of the dining hall, opening out to the lawn and the river below. The sun shines on the "H" painted on the Rock across the Thames. The porch is shady. Harry sits at one end of the oval.

An information officer from Harvard hovers nearby. The group is quiet, until someone offers a question. Harry answers politely, occasionally adding something he was not asked, but he is not effusive. The questions are mostly the typical ones about how the season went and what he anticipates for the races this weekend.

Harry is not enthusiastic about press day. He is not especially interested in what the reporters have to say. He has been misquoted so often in forty-five years that it hardly bothers him. Sometimes, he says, reporters just make things up. This week there may be a story in one or another newspaper for three days straight. Throughout the spring season Harvard rowing is covered faithfully by the *Boston Globe*, with a decent report of each race and regatta (and, it must be said, a respectful devotion to the person of Harry Parker). Eighty years ago they would have sent a reporter in the coaching launch almost daily, describing the technique of each individual oarsman. By the time Harry started, this attention was fading, but the *Globe* might send a writer to Henley occasionally. Harry was not impressed with the quality of their work. (In 1968 the *Globe* published an article titled, "The Further Parker's Jaw Juts, the Harder Harvard Crew Works," featuring a comical photograph of Harry, chin out, mouth open, looking slightly surprised, and describing his jaw as "a noble piece of architecture.") However, there were exceptions. He remembers, by name, two writers at the *New York Times* and one at the *Herald Tribune* who did their research and knew what they were talking about. "The only one left like that is the guy in Providence."

Asked if he is proud to have Penn graduates coaching both Harvard and Yale, Harry says, "I hadn't thought of it," but then declares his allegiance to Harvard and describes himself as "a company man." Asked if this is his favorite week of the year, he says, "pretty close to it." Asked about the direction the race will be rowed, he returns a long explanation of why an upstream race is more likely to provide better rowing conditions. After maybe twenty minutes, the Harvard sports information staffer says, "Anything else? Let's have lunch." Harry eats with the reporters in the screened nook connected to the porch, answering a few more questions, while the rowers eat in the dining hall proper.

Jon Page '02

The 1999 Harvard-Yale Race

That season the varsity crew had not done well. There were only two returning varsity oarsmen from the previous year's crew, Henry Nuzum and Danny Diaz. Nuzum contracted a serious case of mono during the winter and had to take a month or more off. Diaz struggled with back issues and could not participate in all of winter training . . . in short, the crew was weak. Wayne Pommen once mentioned to me that he thought it might have been the slowest varsity crew Harry ever coached.

Anyway, by some Harry Parker miracle the crew beat Brown during the first race of the season. It came down to a couple seats and the experience of the stern pair, along with a favorable home course, no doubt helped the cause tremendously. Harvard then proceeded to get destroyed by Princeton (later the Sprints champs) and then lose the Adams Cup as well. The crew finished with a great race against Northeastern. So as luck would have it, the Brown crew ended up getting faster and faster so that by Sprints, Harvard got a favorable draw. Harvard made the Grand Finals and Yale did not because they had the bad luck to draw Brown in the heats. Harvard got fifth in the Grand, just ahead of Northeastern, while Yale won the Petites. Now, the Yale seniors in '99 had won the Sprints as freshmen and even won the Temple Cup at Henley. They had beaten the Harvard frosh decisively at H-Y. In '97, some of those guys helped the Yale varsity get a silver medal at Sprints. Needless to say, they were very disappointed at being in the Petites.

Now, this was back during the era when wars were fought over the rights to paint the rock on the Thames. Over the course of the week we were down there, there were some not nice things put on the rock, especially by Yale. One choice painting had Bill giving Harry fellatio. Harvard responded by painting taunts about Yale being in the Petites and about having lost by such a large margin the year before. The day before the Combi race, there was an unpleasant altercation on the rock where Matt Milikowsky was spray painted blue from head to toe. To top it all off, the Harvard cox gloated when he defeated his nemesis in the coxswains' race.

Harry, for his part, simply glowed during the week-long lead up to The Race. He was all business. Practices were hard and focused. He knew The Race would be close and he knew that a victory would redeem the season. The varsity race was close for the first three and a half miles. I remember it being within a few seats for most of that time. In the last half mile, Harvard hit a wall and Yale ended up winning by seven seconds or so.

Now, Henry Nuzum is a badass. Old school. And he loved Harry. Loved him like a father. There was nothing in the world that Nuzum wanted more than to win that race. He put it all on the line. Everything. And lost. At the banquet, Nuzum was shell-shocked. He had started his Harvard career by losing to Yale and he ended it by losing to Yale. He literally just sat there with a slight stoop staring into nothing. Danny Diaz was in the hospital recovering from dehydration. Kastner, the coxswain, had taken him there.

After the main course, Harry began to speak. He tried to be upbeat, noting the great season that the frosh had had (the first frosh crew to win Sprints since 1990) and the unbelievable race the JV had that day. He then went on to admit that the varsity season had been a disappointment. He noted that he thought they could have won the Adams Cup and they very well could have won The Race as well. Then, he got emotional. He remarked how this crew had as much heart as any he had ever coached in nearly forty years. He knew how badly they had wanted to win. He started to well up with tears when he thought of it. He sat down and Nuzum said a few words. Very low energy. Suddenly, Kastner barged in the door, full of emotion. He was crying and explaining how he had just come from the hospital where Diaz lay getting IV fluids. He virtually yelled at the frosh that they better beat Yale going forward. Scott Beal gave a touching tribute to the determination of Jason Craw. Craw then got up and started crying while he related the heroism of Beal during the season. Even Adam Holland, if memory serves me, got up and said some emotional words. I can honestly say that I have been to funerals that were more upbeat than that dinner.

As things drew to a close, Harry stood up and spoke again. This time, all emotion was gone from his voice and it was replaced with genuine energy. He urged perspective on the crew and told everyone to be down at the docks at 9:00 a.m. to take them out the next morning. All in all, it was a remarkable meal.

Late Friday afternoon the Combination crew heads out to race Yale. A south wind picks up some waves, but also pushes the crews along. Wayne Berger has kept his 3V crew together, and given the depth of this Harvard squad they face no challenge today. Harvard stomps off to a lead and holds it, finishing twelve seconds ahead of Yale without being really pushed.

All week the Rock has carried the Yale decorations it received last year, the painting rights having been won along with the Sexton trophy for the varsity race. But tonight's victory transfers those rights back to Harvard. And so, just as in his first year coaching the varsity, Harry Parker will awake on Race day, walk across the lawn, and look over the Thames to see a giant red H greeting him across the water. (Some blue still shows around the edges—last night's crew ran out of paint.)

In the morning, the JV and varsity have a short row, largely to deliver their boats to the Coast Guard Academy boathouse, downstream and on the opposite shore, where they will launch this afternoon; they will not need four miles of rowing to prepare to race. The Race Committee have set out flags, anchored every half mile down the course. By early afternoon it is warm and hazy, a light wind blowing up the course.

Harry has been back and forth between boathouse, dining hall, and cabin during the middle of the day. Race preparations, banquet preparations, golf swing, lunch, a final crew meeting. He finally arrives back at the boathouse half an hour before the freshmen are due to race. He wears sandals and shorts, a pale yellow polo shirt, a grey "Empacher" cap. Bill, Wayne, Kathy, and Abigail are already there, not to mention 150 others: parents, Harvard and Yale alumni, and supporters. A large contingent of the 1968 squad have returned, forty years on. The freshman crew launched recently, and they are on their own to get to the starting line on time. Kathy has a pair of miniature Harvard rowing blades dangling from her ears. Abigail wears a very old Harvard racing shirt. A car on the hill plays the live radio commentary through its open window.

Harry and Bill head out to their Seamaster launches. Each is secured with a set of lines to the pylons of the tall L-shaped dock that juts out from the side of Red Top. Harry has contrived a system of four lines to suspend his launch in the square space between the dock and two bare pylons off to the side, with enough slack to keep the boat out of trouble, allowing for wind and tide. He goes through his choreographed sequence of untying, pulling, climbing down, untying again, pulling again, so that he and his guests can board. It is not worth offering to help; he knows how he wants it done. Abigail gets the forward spot, her torso poking up from the hatch in the bow deck. Kathy sits next to Harry while he drives.

In the early years, Harry might have sat in the front where his daughter now reigns. When he began coaching, the normal practice was to have a launch driver, often a student manager, but earlier a man named Peters who was on staff at Harvard to drive and repair the forty-seven-foot coaching launch. Harry would give hand signals to direct Peters where to go. When he finally took the helm of his own launch, he noticed how relaxed he felt, almost as though he wasn't working. The tension of directing the driver, the effort of always twisting around toward him, the constant desire to will the launch into a new vantage point on the river, were all gone. "I almost felt guilty," he says. "All I had to do was coach." (Working with US coach Jack Frailey to coach some national team hopefuls in the early 1970s, Harry drove Frailey's launch, and intuitively knew where to put it. "Parker," said Frailey, "you're the best launch driver I've ever had.")

Downstream, below the sub-base, the two freshman crews are held by the stern at two anchored motorboats, which will reposition themselves another mile to the south for the JV race once this race is away. The freshmen go off, and to no one's surprise, a seriously outmatched Yale crew throws everything into the first half-mile of this race, hoping to shake Harvard. No such luck. Understroking their opponents the whole way, Harvard waits a couple of minutes and then makes a push, taking several seats immediately. After this the margin grows steadily, increasing to a seven-second margin at the finish flags. Their time is within a second of the Combi crew's from yesterday.

Harry and Bill approach the crew for brief congratulations, then motor back to Red Top. Each grabs a delighted parent or two to watch their son's race from the launch and speeds off for the junior varsity race.

Harvard's JV have no interest in letting Yale play for the first half mile. They love their fast start and they use it. Their coxswain is level with Yale's bowball by the time they finish their opening sequence and settle into their race pace. From then on the crew is smooth, humming, and glorious. They must keep it up for fourteen minutes, to be sure, but they get to spend those fourteen minutes watching the backs of the Yale blades, seeing the small flotilla of launches grow farther away as they push those blades farther back. Five lengths of clear water have opened between the crews when they finish. After the last few weeks of frustration, this kind of domination makes all the difference.

One more trip downstream, four miles this time. During the brief stop at Red Top, amid the smiles and applause, Harry surprises the Harvard captain's father with a launch ride for The Race. It is a hot afternoon now, the air thick above the river. The span and buttresses of the Gold Star Bridge, looming high overhead, provide a little tantalizing shade. The coaching launches do not venture under or below the bridge, leaving the two crews and the referee to start the race alone. Harry will have to wait for the first twenty strokes of the race before his crew comes level, and when they do, Yale is in the lead.

Nearly every result this year has shown that these two crews are closely matched. The Yale varsity, like their freshmen, want to make a point early in this race, to bring a flicker of shock and dismay into the Harvard crew in this first minute, to make the next eighteen minutes seem endless and not worth fighting for. Before the first flags go by at the half-mile, the Harvard rowers can no longer see their opponents. They are rowing alone.

This, of course, is exactly what Harry has trained them for. They are stubborn. They can stay strong for four miles. They know they can trust their bodies to go the distance, to respond to pressure at any point on this racecourse.

As with the freshmen, it was no surprise that Yale would attack early. Harry told them to wait, so they wait. Yale starts to fade before the two-mile flag, and at that point, Harvard starts to push. It is not the decisive blow-out that the freshmen delivered earlier this afternoon, but a steady, unflinching grind over the course of a few minutes. Harvard's bow slowly moves closer and closer to Yale's, and then farther and farther ahead of it. With a mile to go they have open water. The varsity, like their teammates an hour ago, enjoy the view from the front, and with this position comes a subtle relaxation and a slightly better stroke, but this is nothing like the JV race. They cannot afford to risk a late surge from Yale, or a mistake of any kind. Harry watches sternly from behind his sunglasses. He is not smiling. Not until they have won.

In the end it is a seven-second margin. Both crews are shattered with the effort. In a few minutes Yale approaches Harvard, the crews carefully maneuver until each seat is level with his opposite member, and they pull together. It is the same arrangement used on the water for swapping rowers between two seat-racing crews, but today no one loses his seat, but rather gives up his shirt. With a handshake and a brief word of acknowledgement, each Yale man hands over a Yale racing shirt, and each Harvard man accepts his due.

Back at Red Top, the crew is surrounded on the dock. The air is pure jubilation. A broom is passed around to represent the clean sweep over Yale, and eventually it makes its way up the flagpole. "Where's Harry?" A turn of the head finds him alone with his launch, methodically tying up the four lines to secure it. First things first.

By the time Harry emerges from the boathouse, the crew have tossed their coxswain into the water and jumped in themselves for good measure. Harry is grinning widely. He shakes every hand, hugs every member of the crew. The celebration widens in its natural progression from crew to team to family, alumni, reporters.

Harry manages to back off and stand in the shadow of the boat bay alone for a minute, watching the joy erupting on the dock, smiling quietly to himself. And then they come for him. "Uh oh, uh oh," he says, as he is hoisted, carried aloft to the edge of the dock, and tossed into the river. He comes up smiling, takes a few backstrokes, dunks himself again, and heaves himself back onto the dock. He stands there, dripping and grinning, then—in response to a call from an onlooker—raises both arms in victory.

A cluster of reporters moves in. He admits to being "concerned" during the race today, but "not worried." How does he feel now? "Life is good." Asked about the water, Harry replies, "very nice, I recommend it." Walking away, he goes back through the boat bay alone, looks around, picks up a towel from the floor, and puts it in the laundry pile.

Glancing at the sky a few minutes later, Harry notes that the haze will soon turn to rain and recommends that everyone get moving or they will all be as wet as he is. By the time the Yale coaches arrive to deliver up the trophies for the varsity and JV races, only the coaches and a few rowers remain at the boathouse. Harry walks back to the main campus and sees some of the men already arriving at the dining hall in jacket and tie, ready for the team banquet. Harry walks toward his cabin but then changes course, going into the dining hall to make sure the tables are set up correctly. He is still dripping as he arranges the three trophies on the sideboard.

The broom has swept away the disappointments of the championship season for this team. The campus at Red Top is awash in relief and joy and a sense of accomplishment on an enormous scale. It is a high kind of perfection. Tonight Harry will cry as he recounts the day, standing in the middle of a horseshoe of banquet tables full of his oarsmen, every one of whom won a shirt from Yale today or yesterday. It is such a dramatic climax, an afternoon like this, that moving on from it could be a shock. But Harry says he is able to "go back to normal life." (What is more normal for Harry Parker than this?) The upcoming pattern—the banquet, election of the captain and other officers, breakfast the next morning, packing up the Quarters and the boathouse—helps Harry process this ending. He and his team continue to act together and work as a group under his direction, and in the light of day, when the docks are away and the shells are on the trailer, they make the natural transition away from the unreal reality of Red Top. The freshmen will travel to Henley in a matter of days. Harry will have more time for golf, to relax on Squam Lake. The fall term at Harvard starts in September. More great days lie ahead.

Peter Lowe '74

From soccer on windy Fridays in the fall, to croquet at Red Top in June as an undergraduate, to road, bike, and cross-country ski races as a young adult, to spirited matches on the golf course today, it has always been great fun to compete against Harry. His legacy of competitive intensity, focus, and concentration remains an inspiration. Three years ago, on the eve of his seventieth birthday celebration at The Country Club in Brookline, Harry challenged me to an 18-hole match to help settle a season-long golf competition that we had begun months earlier. When we reached the 18th green, Harry was on the brink of losing and needed to sink a slippery fifteen-foot downhill putt. As I waited and considered his chances of success to be less than 10 percent, Harry studied his putt quietly from all angles, settled into his stance, took a practice stroke, and then rapped the ball into the back of the cup. With an enormous grin on his face, he walked toward me and in an uncharacteristically gloating gesture swung his right hand up, pointed his forefinger, and stabbed the air between us with an emphatic "yes." His expression was one of sheer glee; I had never seen him look happier, and I instantly realized that I had unwittingly provided him with one of his best birthday presents.

Dave Fellows '74

For forty years I have and still do dream about Harry. We are at a US team selection camp, or down at Red Top preparing for Yale, and I have a race or seat-race coming up, and I am not prepared. Harry is running things and all my rowing friends are there.

Afterword:
The Royal Regatta

Driving home from Harry's memorial service in Cambridge, I reconfirmed the scope of my project, this book. At just after nine in the morning on August 17, 2013, fifty crews rowed past Harvard, having emptied both Newell and Weld of shells and oars. Many were varsity eights from years past, nearly or fully reassembled, or oarsmen clustered by decade or era. They wore crimson T-shirts with a white "H" on the breast, just like the Harvard racing shirt, but with the added initials "L" and "P" nestled between the vertical lines. The enormous banner spread between the balconies at Newell proclaimed, Thank You, Harry. It was a procession fit for a king. Memorial Church was packed a few hours later, as was the riverside tent laid for afternoon tea and drinks ("in the tradition of Henley"). Pimms, berries, scones with clotted cream. Actual tea? I didn't see any.

Between the row and the church service, the whole JFK corridor from the Charles to the Yard teemed with rowers. Sitting at an outside table at the Eliot Street Cafe with a group from the 1970s, I watched clusters of rowers walking up both sides of the street toward Harvard Square. Soon the wide but close-knit world of Harvard, Boston, and American rowing waited at the steps and forecourt of the Memorial Church: coaches from other colleges and schools, rowers from everywhere. Vyacheslav Ivanov, the Russian sculler who won Harry's 1960 Olympic final, made the trip.

The service was conducted by former Harvard rower Jonathan Page, now a Congregational minister. We learned from George Parker that his father made unscrupulous trades when he played Monopoly at home, a fact that surprised no one who had played croquet against Harry at Red Top. George also revealed that Harry's high school classmates chose the phrase "naught but perfection shall be my goal" to accompany his year-book photograph. Charley Butt told of Harry's expertise at the engineering of pinewood derby cars. We heard from Monk Terry '68 about pep talks with no pep, how his grandchildren rowed in the tanks at Newell, and how his daughter cried when she heard that Harry was gone. Thomas Wright '06 revisited a persona from his Red Top skits years ago. Joe Harvey '89 spoke eloquently of Harry as an educator and restated what many have said before, that Harry was the best teacher they had at Harvard.

We sang the Navy Hymn ("whose arm doth bind the restless wave . . . whose almighty word the winds and waves submissive heard . . . who didst brood upon the chaos dark and rude), "Not Here for High and Holy Things" ("the purple pageantry of dawning and of dying days, the splendor of the sea"), and "Ten Thousand Men of Harvard" ("they know that o'er old Eli fair Harvard holds sway"). We heard "Crossing the Bar" ("when that which drew from out the boundless deep turns again home") and the passage from George Santayana's *The Last Puritan* that was read at Harry and Kathy's wedding, and which he wanted read again at this service: "What is there in the universe more fascinating than running water and the possibility of moving over it? What better image of existence and possible triumph?" What brought my tears was Abigail, on her way to Harvard herself in the fall, reading Tennyson in memory of her father.

Afterward the ushers, nearly fifty of Harry's varsity captains, stood in long rows with Harvard oars held tall to guide us out of the church. Saying goodbye to Harry came in stages: a gathering of scullers on the Charles just days after he died; the family scattering his ashes at Red Top; this service at Harvard; and the dedication of a stone wall and monument after The Race the following year on the hill at Red Top, with a view of the Rock.

That day in August, surrounded by those touched directly by Harry and listening to their memories, overwhelmed me. It helped me see the limits of what I could do with this profile. There is simply too much. I never intended to write a biography, and at the memorial service I was reminded why. More than once I heard the view that everyone saw their own Harry Parker over the years. So many years! Rowers knew him for a few of those years, lived through an excruciatingly intense experience of Harry, and then may have never spoken to him again. Or perhaps they created a new relationship later and were able to see another version of Harry. His sons and daughter, his grandchildren, knew another man entirely, one who (according to his son David) roared for champagne as he entered the house. Who was that man? I will not be the one to explore that. I will not read all of his papers, search for his letters, or seek out and interview his classmates, however fascinating that would be. I do wish I had been able to find his famous four-page college philosophy thesis (I tried!), and perhaps I should have had some talks with George and David and Abigail. I have allowed my chosen structure—this single year in the cycle of Harvard rowing—to restrict the scope of the book.

No doubt there are parts of the story of Harry's coaching at Harvard that I have missed, perhaps egregiously so. Some (the first women's national team, the 1984 sculling team) have been described elsewhere. I have tried to weave in what came naturally as the year progressed. The one gaping hole, from my perspective, is Henley Royal Regatta. Henley seems almost as much a part of his identity as The Race against Yale. (Perhaps uniquely among foreign crews, Harvard keeps its own equipment in storage at Henley, to accommodate their almost-yearly participation.) It was at Henley in 1959, after all, when Harry was a finalist in the Diamond Challenge Sculls and Harvard won the Grand Challenge Cup, that Harry had shared quarters with Harvey Love's crew and their conversations led to his being hired in the first place. Lacking a Sprints win, Harry's varsity did not go to Henley in 2008, so it is not a natural part of this yearlong chronicle; and I never spent much time at Henley with Harry, so I cannot write that story comfortably or accurately. In lieu of a narrative, I offer a couple of vignettes.

If The Race is the icing on the season's cake (and not the cheap stuff, but real icing to savor), then Henley is the extra layer of cake, topped with cream and strawberries. For someone entrenched in the world of rowing, Henley is nearly irresistible. Great things happen there, reported every minute or so by a laconic British announcer. It feels timeless and quirky and momentous. One of the best pictures hanging in Newell Boathouse shows the 1985 heavyweight crew, featuring among others the first-ever female varsity coxswain Devin Mahony and the great sculler Andy Sud-duth, outside the boat tents at Henley with the Grand Challenge Cup, which they had just won. It looks as though an official, posed photo had already been taken, or they are still too giddy from victory to consider actually posing. They are laughing, not looking at the camera, relaxed and utterly happy in their elegant dress.

Two years after the events described in this book, the Harvard heavies won the Sprints again, and went back to Henley. Their final in the Ladies' Challenge Plate was a nail-biter, side-by-side with Oxford Brookes University from the Island to the Grandstand, neither crew giving in. In the end Harvard took it by a third of a length. Late that day, after all of the finals were completed, Harry stood by the grandstand and watched two crews as they rowed past the finish line, and then walked off toward the boat tents to find his winning crew, smiling bemusedly and shaking his head.

Everything changes in the Stewards' Enclosure after the last race. A taped-off corridor is created around the edge of the grandstand. A long table is erected in the stands, and workers wheel in the trophies and medals on catering carts. They rattle as they roll along the grass, and it seems disrespectful to the historical objects. "Members and their guests" are now milling about the enclosure, ignoring the river entirely, and the energy is different. Throngs are streaming out to get to their cars as soon as possible; others gather in front of the grandstand, backs to the water, awaiting the prize-giving ceremony.

Just before the awards began, Harry again stood alone near the finish line, reading a sign. It politely explained to spectators that a movie was being filmed that day, and that by standing in this part of the enclosure they tacitly gave consent to appear in it. The movie was *The Social Network*, featuring characters based on Cameron and Tyler Winklevoss '04, members of the "God Squad" from several years ago and Olympians in 2008. The two crews Harry had watched some minutes earlier had been facsimiles of Harvard and the Dutch national team, recreating the final of the 2004 Grand Challenge Cup for the Henley regatta scene in the movie.

Regatta Radio found Harry after the prize-giving ceremony and asked him about the win, urging him to put it in context of the many

Henley victories his crews have achieved. He said simply that each one is special. To what did he attribute today's win—how did his crew manage to keep ahead, in such a close race? Harry hesitated. "Sheer determination," he finally said. "They were really, really determined to win."

In 2013 Harry's varsity won the Sprints again, and so did Charley Butt's lightweights. Neither eight stayed together to race at Henley, but from each crew a four was assembled, and these two Harvard crews worked their ways through their respective halves of the bracket to eventually race each other in the final of the Visitor's Challenge Cup. The heavyweights won, as they typically do in such cases. Harry was not there to see it. He had passed away two weeks earlier, two days after hosting a joyous reunion row on the Charles, and two weeks after following his crews in yet another sweep of the Harvard-Yale Regatta, an unbroken pattern since 2008, the year chronicled in this book.

Bill joked that Harry would retire "two years after he dies," and for years the legends told that Harry would go forever ("1963–∞"), but Harry was not concerned with legends and he knew his time was limited. In his last couple of years, when he spoke to groups of rowers, it was clear he was allowing himself to pass on some perspective, to say what he thought was important about rowing. At the US Rowing national convention in 2011, an audience of hundreds gathered to hear Harry speak. He answered questions, not just about last season, but about his first season. He told the story of a third-boat rower from years ago who came to see him; Harry had trouble recalling the face that went with the name. This man had become successful in business, and felt he had learned so much through rowing for Harry, it was such an important part of his early life, that he wanted to give back. What resulted was the largest single donation the program had ever received. Harry's voice cracked several times while telling the crowd this story. It is important, he said—it has been a vital part of his approach—that every rower on the team enjoys his experience. The balance of his efforts went to the top end, but he coached everyone, he seat-raced for the last spot in the third boat. Just as there was "nothing wrong with being sixth best in the world," there was nothing wrong in being low on the Newell pecking order, if you put your effort in and tried to make boats go fast.

In the end, Harry's message became: The lessons you think you learned from me and my leadership, in fact arose out of rowing itself. And there is truth there, but not the whole truth. To be sure, rowing by its nature instills certain habits, ideas, perhaps even values, but rowing for Harry Parker was not the same as rowing for just any coach. And since so much of the rowing world was influenced by Harry, directly or indirectly, even those who rowed elsewhere were part of his world.

Acknowledgments

The biggest debt of course goes to Harry for letting me do this and taking time to talk to me. I wish I could have handed him a copy in person. Thanks to Kathy for trusting me. Time spent over eight years with Bill, Charley, Linda, Blocker, Joe, and Wayne informed everything I thought and subsequently wrote about Harry. Many other coaches and rowers passed in and out of the boathouse during this time, and conversations and recollections about Harry were just a normal part of life at Newell. I cannot list them all, but Adam Holland, Wayne Pommen, Hugo Mallinson, and Michael Blomquist are perhaps the four I have spoken with the most.

It was a privilege to spend so much time around the 2007–08 Harvard squad (not to mention the several previous years of Harry's teams), who tolerated my lurking presence all year. Though I chose not to name them in the text, here are the 2008 Harvard heavyweight crews, as they raced at the Eastern Sprints:

Varsity. Cox: Joseph Lin, Stroke: George Kitovitz, 7. Otto Stegmaier, 6. Joe Medioli, 5. Simon Gawlik, 4. Edward Schreck, 3. Henrik Rummel, 2. Matt Lausberg, Bow: James Bayley.

Second Varsity. Cox: Ashley Fryer, Stroke: Sam Kenary, 7. Christopher Fuller, 6. Mark Fuller, 5. Anton Wintner, 4. James Canning, 3. William Reuter, 2. Ivan Posavec, Bow: Breffny Morgan.

Third Varsity. Cox: Tope Lanre-Amos, Stroke: Christopher Johnson, 7. Andrew Heffer, 6. Tom Fleming, 5. Georgi Vukov, 4. Karl Hirt, 3. John Stroh, 2. J. T. McGrath, Bow: Duncan Gilchrist.

Fourth Varsity. Cox: Kelly Evans, Stroke: Winter Mead, 7. Matt Webb, 6. Lukens Orthwein, 5. Spencer Livingston, 4. Brad Attaway, 3. Tim Delp, 2. Hugo Beekman, Bow: Noah Bruegmann.

Freshman. Cox: Chris Kingston, Stroke: Benjamin French, 7. Alex Soutter, 6. Kyle Gordon, 5. Anthony Locke, 4. James Hills, 3. Al Renker, 2. Phil Matthews, Bow: Stefan Mihaylov.

Second Freshman. Cox: Ben Massenburg, Stroke: Conner Griffith, 7. Christian Wood, 6. Ryan Bucke, 5. Gustaf Gordon, 4. John Joyce, 3. Danny Pellegrini, 2. Henry Cashin, Bow: Alec Lindsay.

Thanks to all of you.

I am greatly indebted to the many Harvard rowing alumni who wrote to me with their thoughts and memories. Special thanks to Wayne Pommen and Gregg Stone, both for their own contributions and for their willingness to encourage their respective networks of alums to reply to me. Here is the full list: Clint Allen '67, Steve Brooks '70, Dave Fellows '74, Peter Lowe '74, Gregg Stone '75, Hovey Kemp '76, Murray Beach '76, Devin Adair (Mahony) '86, Dan Grout '87, Joe Harvey '89, Scott Henderson '95, Scott McMullin '96, Matt Moeser '96, Sam Brooks '01, Baden Ireland '02, Jonathan Page '02, Wayne Pommen '02, Michael Blomquist '03, Justin Bosley '03, Michael Skey '03, and Justin Webb '04.

Ted Washburn, Liz O'Leary, Gregg Stone, and Kathy Delaney Smith all made time to sit down with me for interviews, and I am grateful to the helpful staff at the Harvard and Mystic Seaport archives. Peter Mallory's *The Sport of Rowing* often proved useful in establishing timelines and generally pointing me in the right direction. Online records kept by row2k.com and the Quinsigamond Rowing Association were invaluable for results of races and regattas, and articles in the *Harvard Crimson* supplemented my memories of the 2008 season. Thanks to Ed Hewitt (at row2k.com), Steve Brooks, Eliot Hodges, John B. Kelly, Igor Belakovskiy, David Parker, Janet Tiampo, Peter Mallory, and Dan Grout for contributing or helping to find photographs.

Many years ago, Barbara Goldoftas nurtured an early interest in writing in her classes at MIT, and in our intermittent contact since then she has always been wise and supportive. Shane Crotty, a fellow student of Barbara's, unknowingly helped inspire me to do this, as did Doug Whynott during conversations at the Beacon Hill Friends House. Dan Boyne offered advice and encouragement as I tried to navigate the world of publishing.

Thanks to Sam Simmons and Jonathan Coulombe at Salisbury School, my brother Damon, my mother Kit Anderson, and especially my wife Jocelyn, for reading some or all of the manuscript and offering suggestions.

In the end, I was fortunate that Bob DiForio knew to pass on my manuscript to Rick Rinehart at Globe Pequot and that Rick, a publisher who knew rowing, was so enthusiastic about the project and had ideas for making it more accessible. For me the journey was long, and reaching the end was a relief and a joy, so thank you for making it happen.

Notes

Introduction

xii. "Sweet and Sour Grapes," *Time*, November 15, 1968.

xiii. "in an entirely different class": H. O. J. Brown, "Harvard's Dramatic Resurgence," *Rowing*, June 1965.

xiii. "impenetrable mystique": Deborah Kory, "Living Legend—Coach Harry Parker Changed College Crew Forever," *Harvard Gazette*, May 11, 2000.

xiv. "as much myth as man": David Halberstam, *The Amateurs* (New York: William Morrow, 1985).

xiv. "wordless rapport": Hugh Whall, "Never Before—at Harvard or in History," *Sports Illustrated*, June 28, 1965.

xiv. "all I have to do is push a button": *Sports Illustrated*, June 28, 1965.

xiv. "walk off cliffs": Rick Grogan '75, in Dan Levin, "Smooth and Rude and Fast," *Sports Illustrated*, July 1, 1974.

xiv. "god to his young men": *Sports Illustrated*, July 1, 1974.

xiv. "Harry waved his magic wand": Bob Monahan, "Harvard Boats in a Row," *Boston Globe*, June 2, 1997.

xv. "a cauldron of pain": Dave Higgins '69, in David Zang, "Rowing on Troubled Waters," in *The Rock, the Curse, and the Hub* (Cambridge: Harvard University Press, 2005).

xviii. "Go until you can't go any more": Dave Phillips, "IRA 2005: Harvard, Yale, Wisco, Army," www.row2k.com, June 4, 2005.

Chapter 1

3. "some sort of aura": Eric Sigward '68, in Craig Lambert, "Upstream Warrior," *Harvard Magazine*, May/June 1996.

4. "doesn't always explain": Gordie Gardiner '79, in Lambert 1996.

4. "he brings confidence in any situation:" Nick Bancroft '63 in John Powers, "Harvard's Old Man River Still Rolling Along without Missing a Beat," *Boston Globe*, May 19, 2002.

4. "Alan Greenspan of rowing": Kip McDaniel '04, in John Powers, "Strokes of Genius," *Boston Globe*, June 12, 2004.

4. "He's deadly honest": Curt Canning '68, in Roger Angell, "00:00.05," *New Yorker*, August 10, 1968.

4. "go for weeks": Fritz Hobbs '69, in Lambert 1996.

4. "master manipulator": Gregg Stone '75, in Jessica T. Lee, "Still Smooth, Less Rude," *Harvard Crimson*, October 21, 2003.

4. "he's the best": Neil Holzapfel '00, in Deborah Kory, "Living Legend," *Harvard Gazette*, May 11, 2000.

4. "most competitive human being": Ted Washburn '64, in Lambert 1996.

4. "the teacher/mentor was Harry": David Fellows '74, personal communication.

4. "send a shiver down your spine": Ian Gardiner '68, in Lambert 1996.

4. "best coach in the whole wide world": Tom Pollock '65, in William Wallace, "Harvard Eight Has Superb Rowing Skill," *Boston Herald*, June 13, 1965.

4. "forged in Harry's fire": Hovey Kemp '76, personal communication.

CHAPTER 2

22. "found a sport that demanded some skill": Harry Parker, Foreword to Barry Strauss, *Rowing Against the Current*, (New York: Simon & Schuster, 1999).

26. "grim and grand as an 1890 railroad depot": *Sports Illustrated*, June 28, 1965.

28. "There is something about that place": Bryan Volpenhein, "The Sickness Unto Next Time," www.row2k.com, March 21, 2003.

33. "still got it": Michael Skey '03, personal communication.

CHAPTER 3

41. "on the verge of tears": John Ahern, "Vesper Beats Harvard, Captures Olympic Spot," *Boston Globe*, July 12, 1964.

45. "all three major muscle groups used in rowing must be engaged": "Parker on Rowing Technique," from John A. Ferriss, ed., "Rowing Fundamentals," The Coaching Resource (Ithaca: The Coaching Resource, 1992).

47. "pull as hard as you possibly can": Michael Skey '03, personal communication.

48. "short, sharp, occasional directives": Wayne Pommen '02, personal communication.

48. "trusting in their athleticism:" Justin Bosley '03, personal communication.

48. Castellano quote: Pommen, personal communication.

49. "Triple Name Call": Pommen, personal communication.

CHAPTER 4

61. Alligator story: Justin Webb '04 and Joe Shea, personal communication.

61. Harvard Business School analogy: David Fellows '74, personal communication.

62. "his eyes were burning": Dan Levin, "Fast to the Very Last Gasp," *Sports Illustrated*, June 24, 1975.

62. "Sorry": Pommen, personal communication.

62. "if we lost": Fellows, personal communication.

63. "looooooots of apples": Justin Bosley '02, personal communication.

63. "calm amid lunacy": *Sports Illustrated*, July 1, 1974.

63. "He knows everything": Ed McNamara '04, personal communication.

63. "more than we thought": Webb, personal communication.

63. Vodka: Pommen, personal communication.

65. "like twins": Ed Winchester, "Deconstructing Harry," *Rowing News*, December 2004.

65. "emulating what he already was": David Halberstam, *The Amateurs*.

66. Talking with the captain: Pommen, personal communication.

66. Teasing intern: Liz O'Leary, personal communication, July 2008.

67. "Simplicity": Joe Harvey '89, in his remarks at Harry Parker's memorial service, August 17, 2013.

73. "too big for that distance": Francis Rosa, "4 Miles to Harvard Crew's Liking," *Boston Globe*, June 13, 1963.

73. "no bad omens": Jim Carfield, "Harvard Geared to Upset," *Boston Herald*, June 13, 1963.

73. "greatest American crew there has ever been": *Sports Illustrated*, June 28, 1965.

73. "shell-shocked": Francis Rosa, "Harvard's Crew Amazes Coaches," *Boston Globe*, May 3, 1965.

73. "the only coach in the East not to heap praise": "Parker 10 Years Ahead of His Time," *Boston Traveler*, 1965.

73. "hard to believe": *Boston Globe*, May 3, 1965.

73. "a soft-voiced, modest, non-blustery type": Victor Jones, "Harvard's 'Wonder Crew' and Its Coach," *Boston Globe*, June 6–9, 1965.

74. "more or less forever": *Boston Globe*, June 6, 1965.

74. "This sport tends to be conservative": "Think. Feel. Win." *Time*, June 18, 1965.

77. "Isn't that great!": in Roger Angell, "00:00.05," *New Yorker*, August 10, 1968.

77. "indeed a remarkable man": in Joe Harvey '89's remarks at Harry Parker's memorial service.

Chapter 5

89. "best-rowing crews on the river": Andrew Dunn, personal communication.

Chapter 6

96. "Alan Greenspan of rowing": Kip McDaniel, in John Powers, "Strokes of Genius," *Boston Globe*, June 12, 2004.

96. "very active": Washburn, personal communication.

96. "your day belongs to me": Bosley, personal communication.

98. Powerhouse Stretch: Nick Peters, personal communication, August 2013.

104. on seat-racing: Harry Parker, "'Seat Racing' . . . for crew selection," *The Oarsman*, July/August 1973.

104. "kiss your momentarily inflated sense of control good-bye": Emory Clark, "Harry's Secret, or—Seat Racing explained!" *The Oarsman*, May/June 1974.

111. "holistic approach" to crew selection: Scott Henderson, Murray Beach, Peter Lowe, Wayne Pommen, personal communication.

Chapter 7

119. "revel in your prowess": J. Adam Holland '94, remarks on induction to the Harvard Varsity Club Hall of Fame, 2007.

Chapter 8

136. "perfect, just perfect": Dave Matthews, "The Lightning Strikes Twice," Harvard-Yale Race program, 1970.

Chapter 9

149. "I'll probably miss this most of all": Jamie Kageleiry, "The Race," *Yankee*, June 2000.

150. "the voice you want whispering in your ear": Liz O'Leary, personal communication.

151. George and miniature golf: *New Yorker*, August 10, 1968.

152. "best emotion and expression": Scott McMullin '96, personal communication.

152. "the Old PF": Fellows, personal communication.

152. "Here, Pika-Pika": Thomas Wright '06, in his remarks at Harry's memorial service, August 17, 2013.

154. "Incredible, just incredible": John Powers, "Yale Stuns Harvard," *Boston Globe*, June 10, 2007.

155. "not so bad we couldn't send out the freshmen": Harry Parker, June 7, 2003.

157. "a noble piece of architecture": John Ahern, "The Further Parker's Jaw Juts, the Harder Harvard Crew Works," *Boston Sunday Globe*, June 9, 1968.

161. "All I had to do was coach": Harry Parker, May 8, 2008.

Afterword

170. "two years after he dies": Bill Manning, in Conor Nevins, "After Four Decades, Harvard's Legendary Coach Keeps Winning," www.espn.com, July 1, 2008.

A Rowing Glossary

Blade. The widened portion at the end of the oar that enters the water and pushes against it. Typically the blade is painted with a pattern particular to the rowing team. Once known as the "spoon."

Boatman, or rigger. Person who repairs boats. Often serves a general maintenance role at a boathouse.

Bow. The front end of a boat.

Bowball. A round piece of rubber attached to the sharp tip of the bow for safety.

Bow-man, or bow. The rower in the front-most seat in the boat, also the "one" position. Since the bow faces the backs of the other rowers, he is said to sit "behind" them.

By fours, by pairs, by sixes. Rowing with only four, or two, or six, members of a crew. Often done for drills or to warm up.

Canvas. See "deck."

Catch. The action of putting the blade into the water to begin the drive phase of the rowing stroke.

Coxswain, or cox. The person who steers and commands a crew, but does not wield an oar. Since the coxswain's body weight is not propelling the boat, smaller is better.

Coxless. Without a coxswain. Nearly all sculling boats are coxless, along with most pairs and many fours. In a coxless boat, one rower controls the rudder with a special shoe that swivels in place to pull wires attached to an extension of the toe.

Cox box. An electronic device that transmits the coxswain's voice and displays information about time, stroke rate, and sometimes speed.

Crab. "Catching a crab" means having the blade caught by the water and pulled down and toward the stern. The handle is then pushed forcefully back toward the rower, out of control, and can cause injury or even the full ejection of the rower out of the boat.

Crew. The group of rowers in a particular boat. Sometimes, especially in America, the sport itself is called "crew," and sometimes an entire rowing team is called "the crew." Rowers do not use this as a verb, as sailors do.

Deck. The bow-most and stern-most sections of a boat, typically flat and enclosed, originally with canvas, hence the equivalent term "canvas." Often this is used to compare how close two crews are: one crew might lead "by a deck."

Double. A sculling boat with a crew of two, hence a "double scull."

Drive. The propulsive phase of the rowing stroke, from when the blade enters the water (the catch) to when it comes out again (the finish).

Eight. A rowing boat with eight rowers. "The eight" could be the boat itself, the members of the crew, or all together.

Engine room. The middle four rowers in an eight, positions three, four, five, and six. Often filled by the biggest, strongest members of the crew.

Ergometer, or erg. The rowing machine.

Feather. The turning of the oar so that the blade is flat. A rower feathers the blade just after it comes out of the water, and then squares it again just before putting it back in.

Four. A four-person rowing boat.

Finish. The moment during the stroke when the blade comes out of the water. At this position the legs are flat, the seat pushed to back stops, the body tilted backwards, and the oar handle drawn in to the top of the stomach.

Foot stretchers. A set of shoes attached to a square plate and fixed into the boat at a roughly 45-degree angle. Can be moved up and down, forwards and backwards, to suit a particular rower.

Grand Final. The last race between the top crews at a regatta, typically with six qualifiers. From the French "grande finale."

Gunnel. See gunwhale.

Gunwhale. The vertical wall or edge along the side of the boat. Traditionally pronounced and sometimes spelled as "gunnel."

Head race. A time-trial in which crews are started one after another. Typically these are longer races with many entries, and typically the starting order is determined, at least in part, by the previous year's finishing order.

Length. I.e., "boat length," a way to measure relative position of crews in a race. A margin might be described as two lengths, half a length, a quarter of a length, etc.

Paddle. To row without much pressure. Also, what canoeists use (but not rowers) to move their boats.

Pair. A two-person rowing boat, or two adjacent members of a four or eight.

Petite Final. A race between the next-fastest group of crews who did not qualify for the Grand Final. Typically this determines places seven to twelve.

Piece. A defined distance or time interval within a rowing practice. Many rowing workouts consist of multiple pieces (or intervals) with short periods of rest in between.

Pogie. A sort of glove or sock that surrounds a rower's hand, with holes to allow the oar handle to pass right through, so the rower can touch the handle directly.

Port. The boat's left side. Also, a rower whose oar extends to the port side.

Power ten. An extra-powerful set of ten strokes used strategically during a race.

Quad. A sculling boat with a crew of four, hence a "quadruple scull."

Rate. The frequency of strokes taken per minute, also called the "stroke rate."

Recovery. The portion of the rowing stroke when the blade is out of the water and the rower is moving it toward the next catch.

Rigger. Properly an "outrigger," the support structure that holds the oar-lock some distance away from the hull of the boat.

Seat. The actual rolling (or "sliding") seat. Also, a measurement of relative position of two crews, referring to the amount of space occupied by a single rower. One crew might be "two seats up" on another crew.

Shell. A rowing boat, so called because the hull is a very thin rigid layer built over a supporting framework.

Single. A one-person sculling boat.

Scull. The action of rowing with two oars per person. Also the kind of oar used for this.

Slide. The part of the stroke during which the rower's seat rolls toward the catch position. (There was a time when rowers literally slid along a smooth or greased deck.)

Split. Time to go five hundred meters. This is the typical number rowers watch on the ergometer to gauge their speed, though actually it is the reciprocal of speed: a lower split means a higher speed.

Square. The position of the blade when it is perpendicular to the water. The rower squares the blade before the catch, and then feathers again after removing it from the water at the finish.

Starboard. The boat's right side. Also, a rower whose blade extends to the starboard side.

Stern. The back end of the boat.

Straight. Without a coxswain, equivalent to "coxless."

Stroke. The whole sequence of body and oar that is repeated in rowing. Also, the stern-most rower in the boat, the one whose stroke must be matched by the other members of the crew.

Stroke rate. The frequency of strokes taken per minute.

Sweep. Rowing in which each rower wields one oar, as opposed to sculling.

Weigh enough, or way nuff, or equivalent. The command to stop rowing.

INDEX

About the Author

Toby Ayer has rowed competitively for more than twenty years. He began the sport as an undergraduate at MIT, then continued as a Rhodes Scholar at Oxford. He was a contender for the US National Team on three occasions, and has won numerous events including Head of the Charles and the World Indoor Rowing Championships. He currently teaches and coaches rowing at Salisbury School in Connecticut.